TRAVELING LIGHT

Traveling Light

Monologues by Jim Stowell

Milkweed Editions

TRAVELING LIGHT

Printed in the United States of America
Published in 1988 by *Milkweed Editions*
Post Office Box 3226
Minneapolis, MN 55403
Books may be ordered from the above address

ISBN 0-915943-31-X
Library of Congress Catalog Card Number: 88-42976

91 90 89 88 4 3 2 1

Publication of this book is made possible by grant support from the Metropolitan/Regional Arts Council with funds appropriated from the Minnesota State legislature, from the Literature Program of the National Endowment for the Arts, the Dayton Hudson Foundation for Dayton's and Target Stores, and by support from the Jerome Foundation, the Arts Development Fund of United Arts, and by the First Bank System Foundation's Small Arts Funding Program.

To my Mother

and especially to the memory

of my Father—

We made it, Dad.

Author's Preface

This book is a strange sort of beast—several different kinds of animals at once. It is a translation, the translation of a work from the language of theater to the language of readership.

Traveling Light was first produced by the Brass Tacks Theater in 1987. The work was presented as a series of monologues consisting of two parts of about one and a half hours each. I divided the work because it is functionally impossible to present three hours of straight story-telling to an audience. The only cross-over story was *Boots, Buses and Bounce*, one I felt was important for each audience to hear. In this book, we have the advantage of gathering all the stories together in an order that seems to work the best.

The stories were developed to be told out loud in front of a live audience. Quite naturally, they changed when they met the audience. I made changes in lines, but more importantly, I altered shading, focus, emphasis and rhythm.

When I toured *Traveling Light* recently, the stories changed again. Each time, in each different circumstance, the stories move around. There was no written manuscript of the show when we began to work on the book. All the stories had arrived at the telling stage in my mind through a process of editing that did not involve writing them down. So, the book-making process started with an oral manuscript which had to be transcribed and edited to make the work as "right" on the page as it was on the stage, and to catch as much of that feeling of live story-telling as possible. For me, it was like going from a land of all curves to a land of straight lines, angles, and corners. Taking what is fluid and pinning it down. In the long, ongoing life of these stories that now go to readers, this book is a frozen piece of time. Or, maybe, a photograph of a river.

Thank you, first of all, to Jessica, and to Jerry and Lorenzo, for all their love. And to Patty, to John R., John H., and to Lois the typist.

—Jim Stowell

TRAVELING LIGHT

TRAVELING LIGHT

Sea Turtles and Pelicans

I am standing on a deserted beach in Vero Beach, Florida. The sun is rising across the Atlantic Ocean. I am watching a flight of pelicans flying around the point in the distance. Five, six, seven pelicans. One right behind the other in a row flying parallel to the beach, skimming above the top of each breaking wave. I am standing on a beach in Vero Beach, Florida, wearing a blue suit, watching the sun rise across the Atlantic Ocean, turning the clouds above me a translucent salmon pink.

A borrowed blue suit.

A borrowed dark tie.

Borrowed dark socks.

Borrowed dark shoes.

I had been on the beach since around midnight but not in this suit.

I came to Vero Beach to help my mother. The house where she and my dad lived was only half a block from the beach. This evening the house was full of relatives, people I hadn't seen in fifteen or twenty years. Around midnight my mother couldn't stand the atmosphere anymore and blew out of the room like a storm cloud.

Once outside, she began to run towards the beach, a half block, on to a trail through some scrub brush, over the sand dunes and then, out onto the beach, right across the beach, and into the water up to her knees. I was following behind, but she didn't see me. When I saw my mother run into the surf, I was afraid for her and ran towards her. She stopped. So did I. She put her hands into her long mane of black hair and began to tear at it. I could barely hear her voice rising above the breaking surf and the wind. I couldn't hear the words, only sounds. I saw her, lit by the moonlight, raise her arms and shake her fists at the heavens. I knew she was cursing the gods. I faded back into the shadows of the sand dunes and out of sight.

She started walking down the beach on the edge of the surf, walking very fast and talking to herself. She stopped, walked in circles, shook her fist, kicked at the surf, and occasionally I could hear her voice rising above the surf and wind. I followed to protect her from herself.

The next morning would be my father's funeral. My mother and father had shared three sons and a life together since they were teenagers. The house was full of his relatives, nice people, decent people, north Texas folks who, when it comes to showing their emotions, bear a tremendous resemblance to Scandinavian Lutherans.

My mother is of a more hot-blooded nature. She had said to me in that soft, south Texas drawl of hers, "Jim, ever since we moved to Florida from Texas and we had to pull our roots out of Texas, it has been this ocean I go to when I need something. When I really need something, honey, I come to this ocean." So she had gone to the water to grieve in the way that she needed to be able to grieve.

She finally arrived at the point, and she was in a position where she could see around it and I could not. She stopped. She was watching something. I could read her body language. She was watching something and then she squatted, and I knew that meant she was going to be there for a long time. I cut into the back of the sand dunes and ran parallel to the beach until I was past the point, then crawled up the back of a sand dune and peered over the top through the sea grass. I knew that with the night and the sea grass, she couldn't possibly see me.

I could see across the beach, and there she was, and what she was watching was directly between us on the beach: a giant sea turtle who had come out of the Atlantic Ocean at night onto the deserted beach, dug a hole, and was laying her eggs.

I knew that those eggs were beautifully white and seemingly perfectly round and covered in a glistening mucus. I knew this because three years before, when my father was still alive, I had visited my parents in Vero Beach. My father and I were watching a football game or something one night when my mother got a telephone call from some of her friends who said there was something "extraordinary" happening on the beach not far from their home, and that she, my mother, "just had to come and see it." I was on vacation and into extraordinary things happening at night, so I was ready to go, but my father said, "No, I'll watch the game."

My mother and I hopped into their new, air-conditioned Thunderbird and drove fifteen or twenty minutes down the beach road to their friends' house and parked. Several other new cars were parked in their driveway. We got out of the car and walked around the back of the house and there was the Atlantic Ocean shining in the moonlight. Every time I saw it, I felt that I had never seen it before. My mother and I stood hand in hand for a moment just looking. "There," my mother said, and she pointed down the beach. "That's them."

We could see what looked like five or six flashlights waving every which way, about 50 yards down the beach. We walked toward the flashlights. As we got closer, I could hear voices and see the shapes of people. Seven or eight adults. Four kids about ten or eleven years old running around. The adults were having cocktails. When we arrived, there was a boisterous greeting for my mother and introductions for me. I was handed a cocktail glass and one of the adults poured me a drink. I noticed that a couple of people were holding cocktail shakers.

Then they all beamed their flashlights in the same spot and showed us the "extraordinary event." A giant sea turtle, a giant sea mother, had come up onto the beach to lay her eggs. The great sea turtles have been laying their eggs on this part of the beach in Florida for thousands of years, long before we came along with roads, condominiums, cocktail parties, and flashlights.

They shined the lights in her eyes and we all crowded around to watch and remark. Remarks like "incredible," "fantastic," "fabulous." My mother suggested that childbirth was difficult enough without having strangers flashing lights in your face and crowding around to stare at you. There was a titter of laughter. I was relieved by my mother's remark. To watch the turtle and, if possible, not even to have her know you're there, that would be all right, but to stand around like this was obscene. The worst kind of voyeurism. It made me feel awful.

We were moving away when suddenly one of the kids, a boy, ran past the great sea mother and dropped to the sand beside the hole, reached down, pulled up one of the eggs, and held it high above her. The little boy looked at my mother; he had obviously done this because he wanted to impress my mother.

"Look," the little boy said. "It's round." The flashlights all beamed onto the egg. "It's round," the little boy yelled, "like a tennis ball." Mutters of laughter and approving sounds were in the throats of the cocktail drinkers.

Indeed the egg was seemingly perfectly round, covered in a glistening mucus and brilliantly white.

I'll never forget the look on the face of that great sea turtle watching helplessly as the little boy ran past her, reached down and pulled up one of her eggs, even as she was laying another one. I will never forget the look in her eyes as she turned her head to watch.

The sea continued to roar in. The waves crashed in the night outside the life of our flashlights.

I let out a groan that could easily be heard above the sound of the breaking waves.

My mother began to speak very fast. "That's all right, honey," her voice calm, but with great urgency underneath. "Please put the egg back, honey. Be very, very careful; we wouldn't want to drop anything so special, now would we, honey?"

The little boy froze. He thought my mother would be pleased. Everyone else was. "Please, honey," my mother said. "Put the egg back."

I groaned again.

The little boy put the egg back carefully.

But my groan broke the feeling of good fellowship for the evening. We stood around and had a few more drinks and talked about how extraordinarily lucky we were. The flashlights flashed on and off the great sea mother as she continued with the work of laying her eggs.

She finished and covered the hole over, trying, as she had all along whenever possible, to ignore us completely. The great sea turtle covered her eggs, turned and made her way towards the Atlantic Ocean. The flashlights followed her and now I could see the water. The same little boy, to make up for his previous mistake, I suppose, ran down the beach and jumped right on the back of the turtle and held up his arms "ta da," like a circus bareback rider. The turtle just kept right on heading for the Atlantic. From the lips of both my mother and me sprang, "No! Stop; stop now. Get off."

The little boy was confused and lost his balance and fell off the turtle's back onto the sand. Zing! All the flashlights whirled

TRAVELING LIGHT

around onto my mother and me. We were caught in the spotlight holding hands . . . and cocktail glasses.

Later that evening – riding home in the air-conditioned Thunderbird, I put down the power windows, *zzzzzzzzzt*. My mother said, "Jim, honey, the AC is on." I said, "I know, but I need some fresh air." I heard her window go *zzzzzzzzzt*, and she said, "Good idea, honey, good idea."

And here we were three years later, and she was watching the great sea turtle lay her eggs, and I was watching her watch.

The laying of the eggs took hours. We watched. The surf rolling in, *boooommmmm!*

The great sea turtle finished, covered her eggs with sand. She turned and started to walk slowly, exhausted, toward the Atlantic Ocean. *Boooommmmm.*

She reached the soft part of the sand. She stopped and dug her fins in. *Boooommmmm.* A wave broke, and the water ran up the beach and under the sea turtle's belly. She didn't move. In the night she might have been a stone.

I saw her lift her head up and look at those waves crashing down on the sand right in front of her. I think the tide was coming in. *Boooommmmm, boooommmmm.*

I felt her take a deep breath and here came a wave. She dug her fins into the sand and pushed off, just as the wave broke, *boooommmmm.*

She disappeared into the surf. I could see my mother turn and watch as I was watching for the turtle, too. Watching the ocean in the night for the great sea mother. We just wanted to see her one more time. Then we could see her. We could see her fins flashing in the moonlight as she swam right over the top of a wave, swimming, swimming hard over the top of a wave and out of sight again.

My mother and I were both watching, watching, watching, and there she was again. My heart leaped out to her, swimming so very hard. She was almost out of the incoming waves, almost out to sea, almost out of sight. We saw the moonlight flash off the top of her great shell as she made it to the top of the final wave and over the top and down the other side and out of sight again.

This time for good. The great sea mother disappeared into the Atlantic Ocean, and who knows where she was going, swimming and swimming. I don't know where she was going. I imagined her swimming all the way across the Atlantic Ocean to England, or swimming south into the Caribbean to islands I'd never even heard of.

The great sea turtle disappeared, and then my mother got up and walked directly across the beach towards where I was hiding. She walked right up the sand dune I was hiding behind. Of course, I knew I had been spotted, so I stood up.

I said, "But, Mama, I was watching out for you. I was hiding out over here." And she said, "Yes, I know," and then she embraced me, and it has been like that between the two of us all my life.

We walked silently along the beach back to the house. The house was very quiet now; all the relatives had long ago gone to bed. My mother said, "Jim, honey, I've got to get some rest. We want to give your daddy a good send-off in the morning." She went to bed and I went into yet another one of a seemingly endless line of strange rooms that I have slept in during my travels and put on my borrowed blue suit, walked to the beach and watched the sun rise across the Atlantic.

By this time the flight of pelicans was almost directly in front of me. The sun was about half-way up the horizon, and the sunlight was streaking across the water, creating a perfect silhouette of each pelican, making their every move incredibly clear. I could see what it was they were doing, flying along the top of each wave.

Right at the point where the wave was turning over to break, at the very top of the wave, I could see each bird, in turn, barely dipping the tip of its beak exactly at that point where the wave was turning over, where the sea plankton, the little microscopic sea goodies, were closest to the surface.

It was at that exact point and that exact time in the dynamic of each breaking wave that each pelican dipped just the tip of its beak to feed.

An extraordinary dance of flying pelican and breaking wave.
One cycle after another,
one cycle after another down the beach,
one, two, three, four, five, six, seven,
fly, glide and dip;
flap, fly, glide and dip;
one cycle after another,

right down the coast of Florida, following the waves as they broke.

Waves and pelican, one cycle after another,

until they were just a tiny, brown, dancing line against the bright Atlantic blue sky.

Boots, Buses, and Bounce

I. Boots

Mojave. Mojave, California. Mojave, a transfer point, and it is hot. Just north of Los Angeles. Change directions north to south, east to west, change buses for Highway 395 north to Owens Valley.

I'm getting off a Greyhound bus, and as soon as I step off the bus, I am slapped in the face with heat from the Mojave desert and the diesel stink from the other Greyhound buses idling on the gravel driveway.

I step onto Highway 395 that runs in front of the bus station, and I can see the sun setting behind the San Gabriel Mountains, at least I think that's what those mountains are. A bright, unnatural, orange, glowing sunset. The Los Angeles basin.

Mojave, heat, diesel stink, cigarette butts on concrete and an unnatural sunset.

I'm getting out of a car in Cleveland, Ohio, and it is night. I have to climb up an embankment off a freeway, and at the top of the embankment there is a ten-foot-high chainlink fence with barbed wire at the top. I have to climb that fence and get to the other side so I can get onto a country road that runs crosswise to the freeway, and then I can walk for one mile on that country road and I will arrive at Interstate 90 running east and west, and Interstate 90 will take me all the way around Lake Ontario and Lake Erie up to the northeastern part of the United States.

I climb up the embankment. Sounds of the freeway begin to fade. I reach the fence and throw my little bag over the fence to the other side. Now I have to climb this fence. The chainlink part is easy. At the top where the barbed wire is, you have to have your coat ready to throw over the barbed wire. Then you climb over your coat. You hang with both feet against the fence, one hand through the fence and you lean away from the fence and peel your coat off the barbed wire. No matter how many times you may have made this move, and at this point in my life I had done it quite a few times, you always get a new rip or two when you peel your coat off the wire. Then you climb down the fence and hop the last few feet onto the ground and fall onto the seat of your pants.

As I put my coat on, I look at the little country road and I realize I don't know in which direction to go to walk one mile to Highway 90. I am in Cleveland, it is pitch black, and it is pouring rain.

And it is at moments like this that I sometimes ask myself, "Jim, where in the hell did this get started?"

Getting into cars, getting out of cars, getting into buses, getting out of buses, getting onto trains, getting off trains, getting out of a taxi cab and then into a plane, and off the plane into a taxi cab, and out of that taxi cab into a bus and off the bus and into a car that will get you onto the back of a truck that will get you out onto the side of the road in the middle of nowhere somewhere. And then I wonder, *where in the hell did this get started?*

My granddad Jim, he lived on a large ranch outside of a small town called Shamrock, Texas, not far from Amarillo, which is in what is called the panhandle of Texas, north Texas. I was his namesake boy, so every Christmas and on my birthdays and sometimes "just because you're my grandson; hell, I don't need no other reason than that," he would give me a very nice gift, but always exactly the same gift every time. Exactly the same gift. Boots. Of course, cowboy boots. Real, leather cowboy boots. If I saw him again two weeks later, he would give me another pair of new boots.

I was eight years old, living in McAllen, Texas, and my Granddad Jim and grandmama Lina, his wife, were visiting. Granddad Jim and I were standing in the living room and I was holding another pair of boots, and I said, "But Granddad Jim, you just give me a new pair of boots two weeks ago."

He looked down at me and laughed. I remember him as a huge man, and that I was always looking up at him. Of course, I never saw him after I became an adult. I told my brother Lorenzo how big granddad Jim was and Lorenzo laughed. "Oh no," he said. "He was a little guy, 5'7," 140–145 pounds, wiry, hard, typical cowboy, no ass, levis just hung off him, his hands were beat to hell."

His voice was a high plains, Texas cowboy, twangy drawl, and his laugh echoed years of riding through north Texas canyons, rolling his own cigarettes with rough-cut tobacco and spending a lifetime in bars and honky tonks.

Granddad Jim looked down at me and laughed and said,

TRAVELING LIGHT

"Jim," he liked to call me Jim because I was his namesake; "Jim, you're going to need every pair of boots you can get your hands on. I took one look at you, Jim, and I could see you got what we call around here that long-gone, lonesome, locomotive look in your eye, Jim. You're going to need every pair of boots you can get your hands on. Just remember, boy, a movin' target is harder to hit." He laughed again.

I never forgot that piece of advice, Dad Jim.

Oh, ya, getting into a Chevrolet. You can see the USA in a Chevrolet; you can afford a Ford if you can; getting into a Pontiac, a car named after a dead Indian Chief; an Oldsmobile, a car named after a dead industrialist; a Cadillac—in twenty years of hitchhiking I got picked up by one Cadillac—one day in Missouri, it was 8:00 a.m., and all he wanted was someone to talk dirty to.

He was talking as I climbed in. The radio was playing the farm report, hog futures, and he was muttering, and murmuring, rumbling, uuuuummmmm, uuurrrggg, his voice rising barely above the radio and solidifying into words I would hear, hump, fuck, suck, and then back to mutter, mumble, grumble, rrrrr and then his voice said, "Where you headed kid?"

"Uh," I said, "north, I'm headed for the Interstate."

"Oh," he said. "You want Highway 52."

"Ya," I said, "that's it."

"Ya," he said, "that's it," and he lapsed back into muttering, uhhhghhggggghhhhhggg cunt, cock, crotch, clit, uhhhgghhggggg-hhhrrrrggg, mumble, drumble, he drifted down into sound like he was gargling nonstop.

The first crossroads we came to, I said, "This is where I get off."

He said, "I thought you were going to Highway 52?"

"No, this is it," I said. "I get out right here."

And as I got out I heard him going, uuummmmmmmmm-uurrrrggggg, shit, fuck, suck, suck, suck, uuuuurrrrrr-mmmmmmmmaahahahaaaah, and as I watched him drive away, I wondered, *how can anyone do that at 8:00 o'clock in the morning?*

Getting into and out of a DeSoto, a Chrysler, or a six-cylinder Dodge. I drive all the way across the country on Interstate 40 out of Los Angeles through Barstow, turn east and drive through Needles, spend the night in Kingman, Arizona, and on through Thoreau and Tucumcari, New Mexico, and roll across the border into Texas.

It's funny. I don't know if I even have a single living relative in Texas any more, and most of my friends are dead and gone, but when I hit the border of Texas, whether I am coming from the east or the west, or if I'm coming down from the north, I enter the state of Texas and I feel like a little fist inside me just relaxes.

I keep traveling along Interstate 40 through Amarillo, past Shamrock—of course Interstate 40 didn't exist when my grand-dad Jim had his ranch out here—out of Texas into Oklahoma City, past the Canadian River in Oklahoma, the Boston Mountains in Arkansas, into Tennessee, to Greensboro, North Carolina, and on to the Atlantic Ocean or, in 1969, traveling all the way across the country going east to west.

I started in Newark, then west on to New Jersey, hitchhiking, getting short rides in the crowded east, into Pennsylvania and Ohio. Of course, you have got to remember, this is 1969, so I had on my clean blue coveralls and my clean blue work shirt with the embroidery around the pockets. This was my fancy work shirt, and I had a big full beard and really long hair. I would see regular cars full of regular-looking people coming and I'd say to myself, "Nope, I'm not even going to bother putting my thumb out; I'll wait for a Volkswagen." I see a Volkswagen bus coming and I say to myself, "Ahh, here comes my ride," and I put out my thumb. The bus slows down, and all I can see inside the cab is a huge mop of hair with a tiny pair of wire-rimmed glasses. The door of the bus opens and inside there are five or six other hitchhikers, and a cloud of marijuana smoke rolls out of the back of the bus. I'm stoned, just standing on the street. A voice floats out of the darkness of the bus: "Where ya headed, man?"

"The West Coast," I say.

"Far out," says the voice.

"Too much," says another.

"Hop in, man," says another voice.

I jump in.

"Hey, man, wanna toke?"

We take off. Through Indiana and Illinois and Iowa, North Dakota to South Dakota, into Wyoming, across the Rocky Mountains into Idaho, out of the Volkswagen bus into a semi-trailer truck, out of Idaho into Washington state. We stop for breakfast at a truck stop in Washington state called "Martha Washington," and we climb, climb, climb to the top of the Columbia River Basin, and I can see below me there the Columbia River, miles and miles away, a little blue ribbon waving, and I can see the highway twisting, turning, switch-backing, corkscrewing down the side of the mountain.

The driver looked at me and smiled. We had been together for a few hours, so, of course, we had told each other a few stories about ourselves.

He said, "Well, Jim, I guess we'll find out if you really like to go fast or not," and *boooommmmm*, down the side of the mountain we roared, with 15 tons of grain streaming along behind, and by the time we finally hit the flats, I was bouncing around inside the truck like a beach ball and we were hitting 110 mph, *yaaaaaaaaaaahhhhhhhh!*

II. Buses

Into trucks, out of trucks, into buses, out of buses. Everytime granddad Jim gave me a new pair of boots, grandmama Lina gave me a toy Greyhound bus. I got bigger; she gave me bigger Greyhound buses. When I joined the Air Force and they sent me to Montana, she sent me picture postcards of the Greyhound bus.

Oh, grandmama Lina and the Greyhound bus! If she only knew how many hours I spent riding on the grey dog.

Pick up Highway 80 in Des Moines, Iowa, and head west through Nebraska into the Platte River Valley, up into Cheyenne, Wyoming; there is always a layover in Cheyenne, Wyoming, on this route. I learned all about Cheyenne in little two-hour jaunts, across the mountains into Utah, into Nevada, all the way into San Francisco. When you get on the bus with people in Chicago and you travel forty-fifty hours with the very same people, very close together, you may not speak to these people for two or three days, but you learn to recognize each other, to take care and watch out for each other in the bus stations and the rest stops. You ride right next to the same person for fifty hours, you learn all about each other.

"Pardon me, I have to go to the bathroom."
"Pardon me, I have to go to the bathroom."
"Pardon me, I have to go to the bathroom."

You find out if they snore. If they eat with their mouths open. You look around the bus along about Salt Lake City and you say, "These people are like my family, a traveling family." Other people get on and ride the bus for 200–300 miles; no, they are like transients. But this is your life.

The bus is different from the car. It's also the same. The same but different. In the car, it is almost always just the two of you alone. And as you travel through the night together, side by side, looking straight ahead, talking, the layers of lives peel away like the skin of onions. Around midnight, men begin to talk about the things they own. "Oh, I own this, I own that, I'm going here, I'm going there, I'm going to be big, I'm going to be important, I've got lots of promise. My wife, oh, we get along great, yes sir," and they wink and nod and let you know that they have a hell of a sex life. And that their son or daughter is great—"Oh my daughter, my kids, I got one daughter still in high school, and she is absolute dynamite, she is going to win this, she is going to win that, she is going to get a scholarship, she is going to go to college, we are really both very proud of her. Boy, my wife can cook this, she can cook that, we're very proud of her."

Along about two o'clock in the morning, layers are beginning to peel away: "I don't know," he says, "about my job. I think my boss really doesn't like me very much. I don't know if there is any room for me. I've got a couple of offers. I can go here, I can go there, I can do this, I can do that, but I don't know—I've got a wife and kid in high school, I'm not sure what I should do." Three-thirty, four-thirty in the morning, the last layer peels away and he looks straight ahead into the limited view of the headlights, gripping the wheel, and the blackness between us is like the wall of a confessional. "I don't know what we are going to do," he says. "I don't like my daughter, never have; neither my wife nor I like her. I tried to talk to my wife about it. She started screaming, got drunk, left the house for two weeks. I thought I was going to go crazy. So we can't talk about it. Nobody talks about it. Nobody likes her, that's the strange thing. So we sit in silence in my house. The silence is growing and growing; it feels like it is filling up every room. When I go home, I feel like I begin to suffocate."

"Actually," he says, "I hate my daughter. We don't talk about it. We don't talk about anything. The only room we talk in is the kitchen. And we are down to a one-word code—*Coffee—Yeah—*

Leaving—Bye. If the kitchen goes silent, too, I don't know what I will do, and I don't know who to talk to about it."

When the sun comes up, everything changes. We start to talk about baseball, politics, farming, his job, why don't I get a job, anything. We never talk about what we talked about in the night. And when I get out, he goes one way and I go another. It is safer confessing to me than it is to the priest back home. If he goes to his priest, preacher, whoever, back in the small town where he lives, he's got to see that person again the next day. Two weeks later at the Kiwanis breakfast, he's got to look him in the eye and know every time he sees him that there is another person in his town who knows that he hates his daughter. But me, he will never have to look in my face again. So he talks to me.

In a car it is the same as on the bus, but different. In a car it's always just the two of you. True confessions. But it's the same, it's time lapse photography intimacy.

Oh, grandmama Lina and the Greyhound bus. Traveling over mountains, mountains named after the wind, mountains named after the blood of Christ, Sangre de Cristo, mountains named after chocolate. Over the big rivers, the Columbia, the Colorado, the Missouri, the mighty Mississippi, the Ohio, the Susquehanna, the Indian and the Big Two-Hearted River, too; and you get on the interstate highways, state highways, county roads, dirt roads, country roads, Hackberry Lane, down to Mill Creek or Rock Creek, Beaver Creek, Badger Creek, Cool, Clear, Coldwater Creek, Rattlesnake and Skunk Creek.

You are always seeing into the backyards, the fragments of backyards of other people's dreams when you travel around in a bus. Riding through Pearson, Nebraska, you look out the window, across somebody's backyard, and you see into the kitchen where the family is sitting down to dinner and the father has got his arm around the son, and you say, "Stop the bus right here; I want to get out and go in there where the lights are warm and golden and glowing and curl up at the base of the dinner table like an old tom cat who has finally come home."

Oh, grandmama Lina and the Greyhound bus. Traveling through Enid, Oklahoma, and you see the old red Oklahoma earth kicking up in the late afternoon wind, and you see seven or eight kids, boys and girls, in a vacant lot playing a scrabble game of baseball, and you want to say, "Stop the bus. I want to get out right here and get out the Mickey Mantle mitt and start to yell, *hey bat-ta, batta, put me on third base, the hot corner, ha, batta batta, hey batta, come babe, come babe, easy out, easy out,* and you want to turn and yell at the kids, *hey kids, hey, hey, we're gonna stay right here on this vacant lot playing baseball for the rest of our lives, because I've been out there and it don't ever get any better than this. Hey batta, hey batta, hey batta batta. Let's hear a little chatter out there, team.* Oh, yeah, because when you are on the road, you want to stop. It sharpens your appetite for home cooking.

But you see, it doesn't do any good. It just doesn't do any good because of the drum beat. That drum beat starts beating, and it gets so loud that you can't hear yourself think, and it gets you right up out of your chair, right downtown into the seat of a Greyhound bus and right out of town before you even know what you are doing.

It was twenty years ago. I was living in Minneapolis, Minnesota, then. I'm sitting in a movie one afternoon feeling like I'm just cruising along. I'm saying to myself, *I've got the part-time job I want, I'm going to school at the University of Minnesota on the G.I. Bill, and for once it is working for me so I have some money in my pocket, I've got the courses I want, the professors I want, my love life is sailing along,* and I am watching the movie feeling fine.

The movie had Joanne Woodward in it, something about a small-town school teacher someplace in the northeast. And at the very end of the movie, I'm sort of drifting in and out of the movie because I am feeling so good, I'm actually saying to myself, *man oh man, Jim,* — I have these conversations with myself, always have— *right along about now, man, it's as if I'm on a two-lane blacktop in a Cadillac convertible on cruise control, and there isn't a single pot-hole,* and I look at the movie, and Joanne Woodward is leaving town on the Greyhound bus. She gets on the Greyhound bus and the drum starts to beat, and she drives off the screen, but I keep right on seeing that bus.

The rest of the audience is watching the movie roll but not me; I'm still seeing that bus, and I'm saying *ya, ya, go Joanne, take that bus to New York City and you can catch a ride to anywhere in the world. Jump on Interstate 90, Joanne, and go west all the way across the USA.*

I'm standing out on the street. I don't even remember the ending of the movie. I go home, I start phoning everybody who has to be called and deliberately not telephoning certain people. Some people are quite amazed, some people are not. Some people think it is really funny. Some people are really pissed off.

I am throwing my few clothes into my bag, and the little girl who is the daughter of the woman I rent from is watching me. She finally says, "You really enjoy this don't you?" That stopped me. I thought about it and then I smiled at her and said, "I sure do."

I went downtown that night, right to the Greyhound bus station in Minneapolis, Minnesota. It has that very strange sign right above the main doors—"Terminal Entrance." Very discouraging, but I go in anyway and get on a bus heading 35W south, right down to Des Moines, Iowa, Kansas City, Kansas, Oklahoma City, Dallas-Fort Worth, Austin, San Antonio, onto Highway 281 south. Highway 281, the road in and out of the Rio Grande Valley, an important road in my early traveling life. Going down Highway 281 south of San Antonio into McAllen, Texas and into the Rio Grande Valley of Texas.

McAllen, Texas, just ten miles from the border of Mexico. I used to look at the map, and Mexico looked so close that I used to think someday McAllen would slip across the river into Mexico. McAllen, named after Mr. McAllen who, of course, owned the McAllen Ranch. We were just down the road apiece from Kingsville, located in the heart of King's Ranch, just to give you a little idea of how things worked down there politically.

Highway 281 goes right through McAllen, Texas, across ten miles of mesquite and cactus jungle with irrigated farms cut out of the thorny bush and over the bridges between a series of levees that were built to protect the cities when the Rio Grande floods. Keep right on going on Highway 281 and you come to the Rio Grande, the International Bridge, American customs, a toll gate across an old suspension bridge and you are into Mexico, and a large city begins immediately on the other side of the bridge, and that city's name is Reynosa. *Yyyyyyaaaaaaaahhhhhhhooooooo!* Reynosa, Mexico, another country, another world. You travel ten miles and you have gone a long way down there.

Reynosa had about 180,000 people at that time. McAllen only had 16,000 or 17,000 people. There was a tremendous amount of traffic back and forth between the two cities. Reynosa was a major city with a huge gasoline refinery. Something of an international city with fancy night clubs, night life and restaurants.

McAllen was not an international city. Hell, half the streets in town weren't even paved until I was thirteen years old. The street right in front of my house, Seventh Street, wasn't paved until I was thirteen and it was about that time that I began my independent bus journeys. Every one of the little towns down there on the American side of the River—and they ran right down the River at varying distances but all were sustained by the Rio Grande—these little towns of McAllen, Pharr, San Juan, Alamo, Edcouch, Elsa, Harlingen, San Bonito, were divided racially. The Mexicans on one side of town and the Texicans on the other.

I would save up my quarters and go over to the Mexican main street in McAllen, Fifteenth Street, and go to the VTC, the Valley Transit Company, and they had a bus going to Reynosa about every half hour. A bus they called the Orange Ball Express. It was not an express of any color. The Orange Ball Expresses were actually old beat-up Blue Bird Special school buses that the American school system had given up on about twenty years ago, and they have been running back and forth and back and forth between Reynosa and McAllen ever since.

I would reach up, put my quarter on the counter, and I would get on the bus with the housewives who were visiting friends or shopping in America, someone's relatives, business men, farmers, and whores. Whores from the red light district in Reynosa who had come to America to buy some working clothes.

The red light district in Reynosa was huge. It ran for block after block after block, with two- and three-storey tall whorehouses with nightclub acts, orchestras and various bands, and an incredibly vital street life of cabs, cars, pickup trucks, horses, mules, donkeys, street vendors, shoeshine boys, gangs of young white Texans, pimps and whores, all kinds of whores. Whores inside the whorehouses, whores outside in the street, whores everywhere in every kind of dress, every conceivable kind of costume you could dream of, and some you would never dream of dreaming up, and almost every age, but only one color, brown.

I started going over there on my own when I was thirteen years old, and I can promise you that I was the only white face on the Orange Ball Express. I would ride over to Reynosa, catch a cab to Boy's Town, another name for the red light district, so that when I was eighteen years old and I joined the United States Air Force because I wanted to go see the world and because they had the

TRAVELING LIGHT

shortest and easiest-looking basic training and because the local police felt it was time for me to go into some kind of institution, I figure I had been going to Boy's Town in Reynosa for five years. So I joined the Air Force to see the rest of the world, which was my dream from the time I was a little child and my parents bought me a globe that you could spin.

I would close my eyes, spin the globe, put my finger out like a pointer on a roulette wheel and stop the spinning globe with my finger touching a country. I would open my eyes and say, "Where we going this time, Daddy?" and my father would look at the place on the globe where my finger was touching and say, "the Sudan. It looks like we are headed for the Sudan, Jim."

"How do we get there, Dad?"

"Well, Jim, we will have to take a plane to a place where we can catch a train. One of those old fashioned steam engines over a very high set of mountains and, oh, I don't know, probably a camel ride."

"Camels?" I would say, "A camel ride?"

My father would bring out the encyclopedia, set me on his lap and open the book in front of us and look up the Sudan, and he would read to me, and we would look at the pictures together. Pictures of the people or of the mountains or of deserts and the facts and the figures, and after a while I began to wonder about things in the world. Things like—what's flax? It seems to be everywhere.

My two brothers who had to babysit me would let me spin the globe. My brother Jerry is four years older than me, and Lorenzo is eight years older. Naturally, then, it was Jerry who had to babysit me the most and do most of my initial teaching. He used to break me in on things a lot. For instance, we would be standing in the bathroom together brushing our teeth and I would say, "Jerry, can I eat this stuff?" holding up a tube of toothpaste, and he would say "sure," remember who he was talking to, and add quickly, "but not too much."

"If I tie my shoelaces together like this, Jerry, will I be able to walk OK?" He would look at me, grin and say, "Sure, come on, I'll race you," and he took off, and I took off after him and fell right on my face. He would laugh. He taught me how to drive a car, ride a bike, things like that.

I would spin the globe with him and put out my finger and stop the globe and say, "Where we headed this time, Jerry?"

He looked at the globe and he would say, "the Belgian Congo."

"The Belgian Congo," I said. "Where's that, Jerry?"

"Africa."

"Is it big, Jerry?"

"Oh, ya," he would say, "very big."

"Get the encyclopedia, Jerry, and let's find out all about it."

"No, no, no," he said, "that would be too much trouble."

He didn't really want to be doing anything with me. I was his little brother, after all. He wanted to be playing baseball with his buddies. In fact, he could see them out the windows of our house, and that served to drive him crazy, but he knew if he told me something, anything, almost any lie, it would set me off day-dreaming for thirty-forty minutes at a time, and he could nip out for a couple of quick innings, and my mother would never know he had been derelict in his babysitting duties.

"OK, OK, OK," he said. "I'll tell you all about the Belgian Congo. Remember last Saturday when we went downtown to the Queen Theater?" That was the name of the main movie theater there in McAllen.

"And we seen that double feature?" I said.

"Yep," he said.

Where I came from when I was a little boy, there was no TV, no TV at all, of any kind. We had serials that went along with the movies. They were about fifteen minutes long as I remember, and they were "Jungle Jim" or "Buck Rogers," and of course, my favorite, "Gene Autry's Radio Ranch." These serials would be shown before the main feature, which in McAllen at the Queen Theater would be a western with Bob Steele or Johnny Mack Brown or Tom Mix or John Wayne or Roy Rogers or Gene Autry.

Jerry said, "Remember that Gene Autry western with last week's Gene Autry's Radio Ranch serial?"

"Oh yes," I said. I loved Gene Autry's Radio Ranch.

Gene Autry's Radio Ranch was about these people from outer space who had landed on the ranch, tunneled under ground, and they were trying, with the help of traitorous humans, to steal Gene Autry's ranch, where he broadcast his radio program from, away from Gene Autry. Even though the bad guys landed in a space ship, they still had to ride around on horses and wear special helmets that made their voices sound like they were talking through tin cans, and they were ruled by this evil queen who had a magic viewer. Anyway, Gene Autry's Radio Ranch had a tremendously complicated plot, but that never bothered me because I followed every episode faithfully. Gene lived on the brink of complete disaster. Every week he would barely escape. I loved that.

I said, "Oh, yes, I remember it. It was the episode where . . ."

"Ya, ya, ya," Jerry said, cutting me off before I got started decribing the latest episode in complete detail.

"Well," he said. A long pause. "The Belgian Congo is exactly like Gene Autry's Radio Ranch." He looked extremely satisfied with his creation, but I was thunderstruck by such a simple yet gigantic idea. I rolled this new, wonderful thought around in my head for a minute before something hit me.

"Jerry," I said.

"Yes."

"Do you mean," I said, "the entire country?"

"Sure," he said. "Why not?"

And I thought, *why not? Sure, why not!* I loved Gene Autry's Radio Ranch. I would love to live in a country where every place you went would be like going to Gene Autry's Radio Ranch. In the wide world there must be a place like that. A place on earth just like heaven. It made perfect sense to me. *Man, oh man,* I said to myself, *as soon as I get older and can get a few dollars in my pocket, I'm going to buy myself a ticket directly to the Belgian Congo.*

When I got older and could read for myself I could see that my brother Jerry wasn't always strictly factual.

Jerry taught me how to drive a car. He had an old Ford coupe with a rumble seat in the back and four on the floor. We would go out driving around McAllen, come to a corner, and I would turn, but you see, it took me a long time to figure out corners. I would turn but I wouldn't turn back. *Rrrrrrrrrr! Wham*, into the ditch. But I was a determined learner so I kept my foot on the gas. *Rrrrrrrrr.* Jerry didn't have the steering wheel to hang onto, so he was bouncing around pretty good and screaming at the top of his lungs, "Turn back, turn around, turn back, turn around!"

"I'm turning," I'd yell, and *crunch, crash*, drive right through the hedge into somebody's yard.

"*Yyyyyaaaaahhhhhh*," Jerry yelled as we went through the hedge. We were now driving across part of their front lawn.

"Are you trying to kill me?" he screamed. "Turn back, turn around."

"What, what, what about my back?"

"You're trying to kill us," he screamed. "You're trying to kill me!"

So he did what he always did in moments of crisis between us; he grabbed me around the throat with both hands and began to choke me, screaming, "You're going to kill me, you're going to kill me!" So I guess he figured to kill me first and take care of the problem that way. I fought back. I took both my hands off the wheel to struggle.

Ahead I saw, right in our path, the house sign of the people whose yard we were destroying. The house sign was one of those awful statues of a black man, a groom, his arm out, and instead of a ring for his master to tie his horse to, he held a wooden sign with the name of the master, in this case, the Terrys. I fought with Jerry with one hand and tried to miss the statue. *Wham*, we ran right over it. Mr. Ronald Terry was one of the richest men in McAllen, Texas.

Wham, bang, we're back full circle, and we are on the road. But Jerry doesn't notice. He's still yelling, "You're trying to kill me, turn back, turn around!" I'm driving with one hand and fighting Jerry with the other and yelling, "I'm turning, I am turning, we're back on the road, let go, let go, we're back on the road!"

And that's how he taught me how to drive a car.

III. Bounce

When Jerry taught me to ride a bike, he took me to the dirt road that ran in front of my house, my street, Seventh Street. Jerry put me on the seat of his one-speed Schwinn, and he asked, "Do your feet touch the pedals?"

I said, "Just barely."

"OK," he said. "You're ready."

He balanced me on top of the bike. It looked like about three miles down to the ground.

I said, "Jerry, what do I do up here?"

"I'll tell you exactly what to do," he said. "I'll give you all the instructions you will need."

"I felt his grip tighten on me, and I knew in a flash what was going to happen next. Oh yes, I said to myself, this is exactly what it felt like before he taught me how to swim.

Then Jerry catapulted me down Seventh Street as he yelled in my ear, "Pedal real fast." *Aaaaahhhhh!* I started to pedal real fast.

Running right along beside me helping me out was my dog Bounce. My dog Bounce. We started together when I was just a little boy and he was a pup and I couldn't quite figure out how to open the latch on our back gate, and when I got older and could figure out that back gate latch, I took off, and he went right through the gate with me into the backyards and alleys, throughout the entire neighborhood.

Now here he was running right alongside of me as I tried to pedal real fast and learn how to ride a bike. He was helping me.

Bark, bark, come on Jim, you can do it, come on pal, I know you can do it. And as I shifted too far to one side to try and keep my balance, the back tire skidded on that old dirt road and *wham, aaahhh-huuuugggggghhhhh*, I hit the road.

My brother picked me up, balanced me on the bike again: "You ready?" he asked.

"Huh?"

"Ready?"

"Oh, sure, yeah," I said.

Zzoomm, I'm launched again. I am trying to pedal real fast and Bounce is running right along side of me barking.

Bark, Bark, come on Jim, you can do it pal, you can do it pal, and I can hear my brother Jerry yelling encouragement, "Come on, brother, come on, brother." *Aaaarrrrrhhhhhh, wham, uuuugggghhhhh.*

My brother picked me up. He didn't run along beside me and try to catch me or anything like that. No, no, not in my family. We had the "get on back up there" philosophy.

When I was about ten years old, my granddad Jim on his ranch outside of Amarillo, Texas, took me out to the corral out behind the barn.

Dad Jim said, "Do you see that horse?" He pointed across the corral at a big roan.

"Yes," I said.

"Well, Jim, that's going to be your horse. Name's Brownie."

I looked at that huge animal. The dust was kicking up in the corral, and I could see Brownie cutting her eyes across the corral at me, sizing me up. Being a working horse on a north Texas ranch is not an easy life. Didn't take Brownie but about two seconds to figure me out, but it took Brownie a long time to figure out that she was my horse. Old Brownie marked me all sorts of ways. Stepped on my foot, bit me, threw me, and accidentally let her hoof hit me in the forehead and left a hell of a scar. Hell, she wasn't even trying on that one.

Granddad Jim put me up on Brownie, and she got me off real fast, so he put me up again, and then I was off again. He'd pick me up and put me right back on again.

I said, "Granddad Jim, gee whiz, this falling off really hurts. Couldn't you try and catch me or something?"

He looked at that cowboy holding Brownie's halter, and they both sort of smiled.

"Oh no, Jim," he said. "It's that fallin' off part that helps you concentrate on staying up there, don't it?" and he would put me back up on Brownie again.

Jerry launched me down Seventh Street. I pedaled as fast as I could. Bounce was running right along beside, helping me. I shifted to one side, then the other. *Uunnnaaahhhh, wham, uuuggghhhh.* Bounce came over, licked my face. *Come on Jim,* he said. *Get up, you can do it pal,* and licked my face again.

After I had fallen off the bike enough times to find every rock on Seventh Street with a point on it, I whined to Jerry, "I will never learn to ride a bike, Jerry. I give up. I quit."

Silence.

Jerry looked at me. "Oh ya?" his voice was soft, quiet. "What's the matter, Jim? You chicken?"

Chicken! Chicken! The word flashed in my brain like a neon sign. *Chicken?* The absolute worst thing that could be said about anyone. *Chicken.* Better to die than be called a chicken.

"Give me that bike," I said. Of course, I must admit there was a very practical side to my reaction. I knew if the word got out that Jim Stowell was chicken, I would have to re-establish my position in the pecking order of my neighborhood, which meant eight or nine fist fights I would have to do all over again.

Give me that bike! And I took off and I was getting better, so that when I fell, I didn't just fall right over. No, no, I would go a little distance, pick up a little speed and then fall *booooommmmmmmmuuuuuugggggghhhh!* Bump, bump and skid along on the dirt road.

Jerry would pick me up and say, "Come on, kid, you can do it, get up," and he would launch me down the road again. *Yyyy-yyeeeeeeennnnnnn!*

I was pedaling and weaving, and all of a sudden I was doing it. I was riding a bike. I was rolling right along and Bounce was running right along beside me.

Bark, bark, bark, come on Jim, you got it, you got it pal, you got it, Go! Go! Go!

And I was go, go, going right down Seventh Street. And I could hear Jerry yelling, "Roll on, brother, roll on," and I did roll down Seventh Street.

Oh, yeah! Now I could see the street that ran in front of my house for the very first time. I had been on it thousands of times before, of course, in a car with my parents, or with the parents of my friends in their cars, but it was different now. The street that ran right in front of my house, Seventh Street, it connected to every other street in McAllen, Texas, and one of those streets connected to Highway 281 north. Out of the Rio Grande Valley of Texas. North to San Antonio, and then north to Dallas-Fort Worth, north to Oklahoma City, where I could catch Highway 66! Highway 66 connects west to Los Angeles or east to New York, and from there I knew I could get to any place in the world.

And as I was rolling down Seventh Street on that bike for the first time in my life, I could see that globe back in my room just spinning around, and now I could reach out and stop that globe any place I want because now I'm the one in control of the wheel. Yeah, Yeah, I'm behind the wheel now, Jack, so look out.

I was rolling down Seventh, and I came to the corner that turns onto Eighth Street, and I cruised around the corner, but this was the first time I had tried a corner on a bike, and I didn't have corners down on bikes too good either, so I went right around the corner, and I just kept right on going into the ditch. *Yaaaaahhhhhhh! Wham, crash.*

But I got better. I worked at it. I practiced and practiced. I got really good. I never forgot how that first moment felt. I got my own one-speed Schwinn. I would get up in the morning, put on my shorts, my canteen belt and canteen, baseball cap (I was a Brooklyn Dodgers fan), and Bounce and I would take off.

We went riding and running. We could go up and down those streets in McAllen, and then we would get off onto some dirt road out into the country. Ride around a few fields, go through an orange grove, circle around and come back into McAllen. We would be hot, so we would pull off the road into the shade of a tree, maybe a big date palm tree, and I would give Bounce a drink from the canteen. You know how it is to give a drink to a dog. You have to hold the bottle up to the corner of the mouth and pour the water in, *glug, glug, glug,* and then I would take a drink. After a little while, Bounce would look at me and say, *Are you ready to go? I'm ready.* And I would say, "Yep, let's go."

Booommmm, back on the bike, back into the street where we would be rolling up and down the streets, rolling and running, picking up speed; now I was riding with no hands, putting my hands behind my back, no problem. No problemo, no hands, and I would be grinning like crazy. I looked down and there was Bounce, and he was stretching out, and I could tell that for him this running was pure rock-and-roll joy. When I think back, I see a little country road, a boy on his bike with his dog.

Bounce's nose is sweeping side-to-side as he is running. I feel my nose open like a dog's, and I can smell the earth being turned over in the Seguines' back garden two blocks away, and I can smell the barbeque over at the Crofts' house, must be half a mile away. My ears open, and I feel like I can hear right through people's walls, right into their houses, right into their kitchen conversations.

We are rolling along when we suddenly come around the corner, and here is a street we have never been down before. I look down at Bounce; he looks up at me. "What's down this street? Big tough dogs? Umm? Maybe? Yeah? Big tough kids? Ummm? Big tough kids on real fast bikes with real tough dogs? Ummmm?" We looked at each other and looked back down the street. A street we have never been down before. Our eyes meet. Bounce's tail starts to wag and I start to laugh. *Yaaaahhhhh.* Down that street we go, full speed ahead.

And as we start down this street, I realize that this is what we have been looking for. This is what we have been looking for all day. A street we have never been down before. Yeah. For Bounce and me, this is all we could ever have expected, all we ever really wanted, all we could ever have hoped for. A street we have never been down before.

Boots, buses, and Bounce.

The Golden Temple

Climbing into a semi-trailer truck outside of Fort Worth, Texas. I'm headed for San Antonio and the Rio Grande Valley. I climb into a semi-truck cab and look at the driver. He is a large beefy young man with a very red face, and he has been on the road a long time. He has those road-map eyes. He looks over at me, slams the truck into gear and we roar away as I am barely in the truck.

He yells at me, "For God's sake, talk to me." *Pow, boom,* down the road we go. Our entire conversation had to be screamed because of the noise of the truck engine, and we talked as fast as we drove. A break-neck pace. Musically, it was like being in a drum solo from the jazz classic "Cherokee."

I yelled, "What's the matter with you?"

"I gotta stay awake, man, I gotta stay awake. That's why I picked you up, even though you look like a goddamn hippie."

He pushed through the gears. "You-got-to-help-me-man. I've-been-on-the-road-for-50-hours. I-got-to-get-all-the-way-to-San-Anton,-get-this-truck-unloaded-and-back. Gotta-keep-going-so-I-can-make-the-goddamn-bank-payments-on-this-rig-of-mine.

And as he was talking at this incredibly high speed, his head was slowly dropping and his eyes were drooping closed. He was falling asleep at the wheel, and at the crucial point, his arm flew up and whack, slapped himself in the face. "Aaaahhhhh," he groaned and snapped back awake and stepped on the gas.

"I-can't-take-those-pills,-they-make-me-sick. They-drive-me-crazy,-talk-to-me, talk-to-me-about-anything-goddamn-it."

"All right, all right," I said. My brain was racing. What in the hell could I talk to this redneck about? Books? Politics? Ideas? "Hey man," I said, "let's talk about baseball."

"I-hate-baseball,-I-hate-it."

"What?" I asked, "what do you mean? How can you hate baseball? That's un-American."

"I-hate-it. Look-at-me. I'm-a-short-squatty-guy,-always-have-been. That-means-they-always-made-me-play-catcher."

His head was dropping again. I watched, fascinated, like

watching a snake. *Whack,* he slapped himself awake again. "Aaaahhhh," he groaned. *Zoooom,* he increased speed again.

"The-goddamn-ball-was-always-knocking-the-shit-out-of-me-and-them-fanatics-sliding-in-and-knocking-the-shit-out-of-me. I-hate-baseball-so-don't-talk-to-me-about-baseball."

"Football," I screamed.

"No-I-hate-football."

"I know, I know," I said, "look at you, they made you play center didn't they?"

"Yes-yes-yes,-they-did-and-on-every-play-they-beat-the-shit-out-of-me-and-they-would-pile-on-top-of-me-and-no-one-could-see-anything-I-was-doing-so-I-never-got-laid-by-any-of-the-cheerleaders. I-hated-playing-football."

His head was dropping again, and, *whack,* again another slap. His head snapped up, his eyes wide open. *Zoooommmm.* He increased speed.

"What in the hell are you doing, man? You must be crazy." I was afraid by now.

"What-do-you-mean,-crazy?"

This job is killing you, driving you crazy."

Oh,-no," he said, "you-have-never-worked-at-a-desk-job-not-you-oh-no. You've-never-had-anyone-looking-over-your-shoulder-every-second."

"Looks to me as if the bank is looking over your shoulder every second right now."

"Oh-no," he said, "oh-no-it's-not. I'm-a-free-man-out-here. There's-no-bank-clerk-in-this cab-right-now. If-one-of-those-idiots-in-those-tin-Japanese-cars-tries-to-drive-under-my-wheels,-who-saves-them? No-bank-clerk,-I-do. If-something-breaks-down-on-this-truck,-who-fixes-it? I-do-not-some-clerk. Out-here-I'm-a-free-man. This-is-my-kingdom. I'm-in-control,-moment-to-moment-to-moment-I'm-in-control."

I said "that's just like Zen Buddhism." I was into that then.

"What-,what-do-you-mean? Buddhism?"

"Yeah, you're in control, moment to moment to moment. That's just like Zen Buddhism. That's like a Zen Buddhist Monk. They live moment to moment to moment."

"You-mean-this-truck-cab-is-like-my-Buddhist-temple?"

"Yes," I screamed, "yes, your truck is like a Buddhist temple."

"Oh yeah", he yelled. "I-knew-a-guy-when-he-retired-he-got-the-entire-inside-of-his-cab-done-in-gold-leaf."

"That's right, that's right," I said. I screamed, "he had a golden temple."

TRAVELING LIGHT

"I-can-do-that,-I-can-do-that," the truck driver screamed. "Cover-the-entire-inside-of-my-cab-with-gold-my-own-golden-temple-all-those-years-I-have-been-breaking-my-ass-to-pay-off-this-truck-driving-myself-nuts-I-have-been-living-like-a-Zen-Buddhist-monk-and-I-have-been-buying-myself-my-own-Golden-Temple."

"Yes, yes, yes."

"Oooooohhhhhhhhooooooo. Yeah-I-like-that,-I-dig-this-crazy-Zen-shit."

And we drove all the way to San Antonio, Texas, talking about Zen Buddhism.

The Devil in Wallace, Idaho

I am standing beside the highway in Coeur d'Alene, Idaho, which is in the northern panhandle of Idaho. I feel good. I have been hitchhiking all the way from Seattle, Washington, and I am returning to Great Falls, Montana, where I am stationed in the United States Air Force. This is only the second major hitchhiking trip of my life. I've just turned twenty years old, and I have $50 in cash tucked away in my sock. I am on leave, and I am not in uniform. I am wearing my civilian clothes. Civies. Actually, some of the clothes I have on are left-overs from Texas, which I left a little over eighteen months ago.

I feel good because I just got a long ride to Coeur d'Alene, and when you are hitchhiking, there ain't nothing like a long ride to pep you right up. I got a ride all the way across the Moses Lake Desert into northeastern Washington State, into and through Spokane, a major city and therefore a point of destination. You can get hung up in cities and have to walk for miles, which wastes a lot of time, is hard work, and dangerous; and, there are always more police around cities. This ride went right through Spokane, all the way to Coeur d'Alene, Idaho.

Of course, it wasn't the dream ride or anything like that. It was in a beat-up old pick-up truck that boiled over about six times crossing the Moses Lake Desert, and the back of the truck was full of manure. Natural fertilizer, the pick-up truck owner called it.

"What?" I asked.

"Pig shit," he said, and grinned, so there was no riding in the back of that truck.

And there was a huge German shepherd who insisted that he was going to ride with his head out the truck window to get whatever air there might be, and that meant he had to ride right next to the door, and if I tried to stick my head out the window because the inside of the truck was like an oven, that meant I crowded him, so he would turn his head, which was about the size of a grizzly bear's, look at me, give a low, powerful, rumbling growl, and I would sit back.

The driver would just look at me and give me a sweet, sickly sort of smile. He was an old, tiny, dried-up gnome of a guy, and though the back of the truck was full of baking, bubbling pig shit, the guy next to me stank even worse. This old guy looked like a nobody, but he was actually an Olympic-quality stinker. If there was a gold medal for stinking, this guy would win in a walk.

For a stink of this magnitude, I thought, I should have an exact name. I had a lot of time crossing the Moses Lake Desert wedged between him and a huge German shepherd to think about it in great detail. I never could come up with an exact smell name. It was a blend of all the bodily functions of several animals, including humans, and, of course, a healthy dose of the stink of blood and death. So I sort of settled on dead pig shit, just to have some kind of a name.

By the time I got out of the truck in Coeur d'Alene, Idaho, half of my body smelled like sweaty dog and the other half smelled like sweaty dead pigs, but the people passing by in their cars didn't know that yet.

I had my map out, planning how far I would go if I got a ride for three hours or four hours or five hours. The old timers had always told me the way to do things: Always get a ride before dark, they said. Don't get let off in the middle of nowhere in the middle of the night. You got to plan ahead, kid; which was a pretty radical idea for me at that point in my life.

I looked up. Cars are zooming by. It was late afternoon, but I was hot, hot, hot. I gave myself an encouraging thought: I just got a ride here, didn't I? I would stick my thumb out every now and then, but I was really figuring out my night trip strategy, because any minute now I was going to get serious about hitchhiking, and then I was going to get a ride.

I put away my map, stuck out my thumb. Here comes a car driven by a single woman. I put my thumb down because I thought then, and I think now, that a single woman should not pick up a hitchhiker, so pass right on by, *passale*.

Here comes a single guy in a pick-up truck. That's a good deal. He's a big, burly guy with a beard and a pick-up truck, so he has no reason to be afraid of me. He could break me like a twig. He goes right on by, *rrrrroooooommmmmm!* I think: a single guy like that ought to pick me up, you know? What's he got to be afraid of?

Ahh, here comes a nice family. Yes, I see a kid in the back seat. "Listen to me," I say to them. "Read my lips. I'm a nice middle-class boy. I'll talk to your kid, or I won't talk to your kid. I'll talk to you. I won't talk to you." *Rrrrooooommmm,* they go by.

Here comes a family in a Pontiac. "Hey, listen, my father used to own a Pontiac, so you should give me a ride." *Rrrrooommmmm,* right on by.

The day wears on, and I'm not getting a ride. The pressure starts to build as sundown creeps closer and closer. I don't look like a bad guy standing here now in the afternoon sunlight, but come nightfall, I transform instantly into Count Dracula. It is a quantum leap in difficulty to get a ride after dark, so I creep closer and closer to the highway because I want to be sure to make eye contact.

I get closer and closer until my foot is right against the edge of the asphalt. I am not actually standing on the road, so that if the Highway Patrol pulls up I can point to my foot and say, "What do you mean standing on the road? I'm not standing on the highway." I'm as close as I can get to the highway without actually being in it so I can be sure to make eye contact. I lean right into the road and then throw my arm out into the road. You couldn't pass by unless I move my body out of the way. This is what I called my bull fighter's hitchhiking stance.

By the time I reached this point, I was yelling directly at the cars. "Give me a ride, Goddamn it!" I would yell. "Give me a ride! What in the hell are you afraid of? I'm harmless!" *Zzzzooommm.*

More cars keep going right on by. The sun got closer to the horizon. I was in the twilight shadows now, saying, "Please give me a ride, pretty please, with sugar on it. I see you've got your wife with you. So what. Stop anyway. What in the hell do you think I am going to do? Jump her? Are you kidding? I've got better things to do with my time than that." *Zzzzoooommmmm,* right on by.

I begin yelling incoherently at cars going in either direction. "*Aaaaahhhhhhyyyyyyyaaaaahhhhh!*" and I'm jumping up and down beside the road, waving my arms, chasing cars up and down the road, throwing small pebbles at them, giving the finger to anyone who even thinks of looking at me, screaming, "What in the hell are you afraid of, what are you afraid of? I'm harmless, give me a ride, Goddamn it, or I'll kill you!" *Zzzzoooommm*, right on by.

Hitchhiking tip number one. Anger and threats never work to get you a ride.

All right, I think, during a lull in the traffic which is starting to thin out as the day grows older. Anger isn't working. Being a normal guy isn't working either. Nothing is working so I'll try something new.

I roll the sleeve of my windbreaker down over one of my hands. I'm a one-handed person. I made sure the cars could see I had only one hand. "How about this," I said. "Come on, here's a one-handed person hitchhiking. Surely you'll give a ride to a one-handed person." *Zzzzzoooommmmm*. One car after another passed me by. They didn't seem to care that I was a poor, one-handed person. All right then.

No hands. I rolled the other sleeve over my other hand. Hitchhiking with stumps. I was yelling at the cars as they approached and zoomed by. "OK, OK, look at this." I would wave my arms around. "Look at this: I got no hands here. No hands here. You are probably wondering how I got out here." *Zzzzoooommm*.

"All right," I said. "Not good enough, huh." I took a shirt out of my bag and stuffed it up under my coat so it gave me a hump back. "How about this," I said. I started to limp and drag my leg. "How about this," I said. "A guy hitchhiking with no hands, a hump back, and a wooden leg. Who could be safer than that? Gimme a ride." *Zzzzzoooooommmmm*.

Hitchhiking tip number two. For me, the sympathy ploy never worked either.

The sun set. Darkness.

So what the hell, I think. I am standing in the light of a street light, a dark shadow hitchhiking. What the hell. Have some fun. I get down on my knees like I am praying for a ride, but I have got to admit, I'm not truly praying, although sometimes I do end up praying. Praying sort of sneaks up on me.

I would see a car coming, which was easy now because the cars were far and few between. "Oh," I'd say, "I'll break my prayers for just a moment and stick my thumb out. I don't care if you stop or not, brother. I've got my prayers." *Zzzzzoooommmm*.

Another car. "Hallelujah, brother, I don't care if you stop or not. Remember this one thing though; we are all washed in the

Blood of the Lamb. Go right on by. Go straight to hell, do not pass go." *Zzzzoooommm*. More prayer.

Here comes another car. "Well," I said, "I just want to say, Brother," and this car stopped. I am dumb-struck. I can't get up. The car door opens; a gentle voice from the darkness of the car says, "Come on, son, hop in."

I do. I forget the three-hour plan, the four-hour plan, the five-hour plan. I don't care where he is going. I don't care if he lets me off in Dead Dog. I've got to get out of here. I feel like I am jinxed or cursed. *Vvvvvrrrooooommm*, off we go.

It turns out he is going to Wallace, Idaho. A great ride. All the way across the panhandle of Idaho. He asked me where I was going, where I was coming from, how long I had been waiting for a ride.

"Oh, about half my life," I said. And I asked him to tell me about Wallace, Idaho.

I couldn't see the driver. There were no lights in the car and we were in the country. He was a talking silhouette. A gentle but strong voice. No real accent of any kind. Old, but clear. Not a whisky and tobacco voice.

"Wallace is a lumbering town," he said, "full of lumber people, lumber mills, lumberjacks." A long pause then. I could see him studying me, and I wondered if he could see me any clearer than I could see him.

"Well, son, Wallace is a wild and evil town, full of evil people, doing evil things." At that moment a car went by in the opposite direction, and in its passing headlights I could see the driver for a flash, a white collar around the front of his throat.

I said, "Is that right, father?"

"Yes. I am a priest, and Wallace is my parish. Has been for forty years, so when I say to you that Wallace is an evil town, full of evil people, doing evil things, I know whereof I speak."

Well, well, well, I think. An evil town, people doing evil things, ah? Sounds very interesting. I'm a young man, just turning twenty, I'm on leave, I've got $50 in cash. I'm having one of those experiences I've always heard about.

I ask, "What kind of evil things are there, father?"

"All kinds," he says.

"Oh, no."

"Oh, yes," he says. "Gambling."

"Oh, no," I say. I think, well, I'm not much of a gambler, but wherever there's gambling, there's girls.

"Yes," he says. "Gambling, drinking, after-hours bars."

"Oh, no," I say.

"Oh, yes," he says. "In fact, the bars never seem to close."

"Incredible," I say.

"Yes," he says, "and houses of prostitution."

"Oh, no."

"Oh, yes," he says. "Often you find gambling, drinking, and the houses of prostitution all together."

"That's simply incredible," I said. "I'm glad you told me that, father."

He looked at me. Another long pause. He grunted. "Uh, huh."

As we pulled into Wallace, he gave me a few more warnings which basically added up to, get out of town fast, kid, but uttered without much real hope, and I am thinking as I hop out of his car, Wallace, huh, sounds like a hellova town. Maybe I'll stick around, blow my $50.

But as soon as my feet hit the road, the drum starts to beat. I'm ready to catch a ride. I forget all about the sin palaces, and I'm ready to go back on the road. I'm hot, hot, hot. I'm going to get a ride. I just got a ride here, didn't I?

I stick out my thumb. There is no traffic. Absolutely nothing, but I am ready. I check out my surroundings. The road runs out of sight into the night up the side of the mountain towards Lookout Pass, over and down into Montana. I am on the outer, eastern edge of town, standing, looking at the buildings around me. A few stores, a shoe store, car parts, and, right behind me, a filling station that's going to be open all night. I can see a kid who looks about my age who is working the graveyard shift, sitting with his feet up on the desk, studying a *Playboy* magazine. The fluorescent filling station lights spill down over onto the road. That's good.

The road in front of me comes around a gentle curve. That means semi-trailer trucks will have to downshift. That's good. Those big semis have sixteen forward gears, and once they get up speed into gear sixteen, it takes them a long time to work down to stop and go again, so they don't stop for hitchhikers once they get into gear sixteen, and if you don't know that, you learn fast when you are standing beside a highway somewhere and a big semi rolls by at 70 miles per hour and it kicks up the dirt beside the road and, wham, you get a sandblaster complexion job.

There's a little curve, so they have to slow down. Trucks and cars. A little light so they can see me. The slower they go, the better they can see me. The better they can see me, the better chance I have of getting a ride. This is a damn good place to hitchhike from. Oh, yes, I'm going to get a ride with the first car to go by, or with a big semi-trailer truck rolling all the way over Lookout Pass to Great Falls, Montana. Oh, ya. A big, warm semi-trailer truck. All right. I'm ready. I'm bouncing up and down on my toes.

Nothing, No cars, no trucks, motorcycles, bicycles, stage coaches, nothing. And as I am waiting, I am having a conversation with myself out loud. I have always done this. Had conversations out loud. I spent many hours of time waiting beside the road having hard and honest dialogue with myself. I wasted a lot of that time, too. Just now, I was walking up and down by my bag, using it as my anchor point.

Hey Jim, I said to myself, *how about this, huh. Here you are in the Rocky Mountains of northern Idaho. You've just been to the World's Fair, the World's fucking Fair. What would those bozos back in the Rio Grande Valley say if they heard you'd been to the World's Fair? Ate dinner in the Space Needle. Who would have ever thought back in the Rio Grande Valley, back in McAllen, Texas, that you would ever be here. Yeah, it's a lot different in the mountains than it is down in the valley. For one thing, it is cold as hell up here.*

Oh, another voice answered in my head, *you're just now catching on to that; you've been standing here congratulating yourself so long you didn't even notice how goddamn cold it is wearing the clothes you wore back in the Rio Grande Valley. When are you going to grow up and leave that place behind? Look at you. It's been well over a year, and all your civilian clothes are left-overs from where you came from. You're a basket case. Now get smart, get smart boy, and get your ass up to that all-night filling station and talk to that filling station attendant.* I said, *I don't know him. What can I talk to him about? I can stay here.*

Oh, no, the voice said, *maybe you can but I can't. Look at what he's reading. See, you do have a common interest.*

I went up to the filling station, bought two bottles of Coca-cola out of the old Coca-cola machine, and went inside to warm up.

We talked, and he said in a slow country drawl, "Sure, I don't care if you warm up in here. Just don't get me into trouble with the customers or chatter away at me."

"It's a deal" I said.

"Fine." Zip. Up with the magazine.

"That's cool," I thought. "I don't want to talk to him, either."

So that's what I do. I come in; I warm up. As soon as I get warm, I go back down to the road. Nobody is passing, but it is my job when I'm on the road that I've got to be ready, man.

Over the next few hours a couple of cars zoom by. About 3:30 a.m., I had just come up to the filling station and was warming up. This was before filling stations had those little things in the driveways that you drive over and ring, *bbbiiinnnngggg*, so a car pulls into the filling station and the attendant doesn't hear it.

He is sitting with his feet on the desk and his face glued to the *Playboy* magazine. I am watching the empty station and the road. A 1940s style two-tone maroon Mercury glided silently up to the pumps. In the fluorescent filling station lights, the two-toned Mercury gleamed. We all sat. No one moved. I could see into the car, and I could see that there was only one person. A man. But I couldn't see his face because he had on a wide-brimmed hat. I finally said, "Hey, a car."

The filling station attendant dropped his feet to the floor and stood up. "Jesus H. Christ," he said. "Where did that car come from? How long has it been sitting there?" He was on the move out the door and was muttering to himself, "like it popped out of nowhere."

I slipped out the door behind him and drifted over by the garage. It was closed at this time of night, so I was sort of hanging out over in the shadows, from where I saw the guy get out of the car and turn and talk to the filling station attendant. He turned and looked across the filling station directly at me.

He began to walk towards me. I could see he was wearing a very nicely cut maroon suit, not double-breasted, pleated pants, vest, silk tie, and hat with a brim, which was very unusual in those days, the early 1960s, and very highly polished shoes. Even though I could tell by his walk that he was older man, he still had a roll and spring to his gait, like he might have been an ex-middle-weight boxer.

He walked directly up to me. He was slightly shorter than me. He looked up at me and our eyes met. His eyes were coal black, with a tiny beam of white light like a window. Then his eyes were like water. Like water where you look when the sun hits the water and there are dancing diamonds of light, and you can't quite look directly at the light but you don't want to look away. I heard his voice roll out of some unfathomable depths.

"I know who you are. I know what you want. I know where you are going. Get in the car, and I will take you there."

The gears of my brain started to strip. The most mysterious part of the entire thing was that I had never seen this man before in my life, and every word he was speaking I knew to be true. I knew he was speaking the truth when he said he knew who I was, knew what I wanted, knew where I wanted to go, and would take me there. His voice rolled on. "I know who you are. I know what you want. I know where you are going. Go now and get in my car."

He pointed at the shining Mercury. But his eyes drew me back again. "I'm going to the restroom and when I come out, we will go to your destination," and I felt him increase the current, the power of his eyes, "together."

He turned around and walked away. He walked inside the station. I bent over to pick up my little bag. I was going to get in the car. Even though he was gone, all I could see were his eyes.

I picked up my bag, and as I straightened up, my eyes drifted up and I saw the stars shining above the Rocky Mountains. Sometimes in the mountains the stars seem so close you can reach right up and touch them. I thought, Gee, I don't remember the stars seeming so close down in the Rio Grande Valley, and then I remembered when I was a little boy lying in my backyard with my two older brothers down in McAllen, Texas. We would lie on our backs, our heads almost touching. Each of us looking upwards. Our children's voices telling what we were going to do when we grew up. Telling our stories to the stars.

Then I began to run. I didn't know where I was going. I had never been to this town before in my life. I just had to run away from that man because he terrified me. I had never been so afraid in my life.

I ran around the back of the filling station, and there was this enormous pile of empty used tires stacked up against the back wall. It must have been forty feet long, all the way across the entire back wall, fourteen feet high, up to the top of the back wall. Thousands of empty used tires.

I didn't think. I dove into this enormous pile of used tires and started to dig for the bottom of the pile. Dig, dig, all the way to the bottom of the pile into the back corner I crawled, covering my trail behind me like a wild animal. I reached the corner. I turned and faced outward, and I waited for him to come, to search for me. I waited and listened.

But nothing happened.

I said to myself, *What in the hell are you doing in the bottom of these tires, Jim? He's just a little old man. You have been on the road too long, Jim, my boy, and you just got spooked. Climb up out of these Goddamn tires, Jim.* I started to move, but then I remembered his eyes and I froze, and I said, *Oh, Jim. I hate to tell you this, but to be perfectly honest with myself, if that wasn't looking into the eyes of the devil, then that is as close as I ever want to come.*

I had never seen eyes like that before. Oh, yes, I had. Not exactly the same, but I remembered those other eyes. The only other eyes I had ever seen in my life with the kind of power, but those eyes were different. They were like looking into a freight train beam of light. The train headlights shining on a bunny rabbit caught on the tracks, too late.

Oh, yeah, I remembered those eyes. I saw them outside Biloxi, Mississippi, and it had been almost exactly one year before, just outside Biloxi, Mississippi, and I was returning home to McAllen on leave from the United States Air Force. I had joined the Air Force when I was 18 years old, and they sent me to computer school in Biloxi, Mississippi.

Blowing up a basketball was a complex mechanical act for me, so of course the Air Force put me immediately into computers. I was there eight or nine months. In school I worked with computers, and in basic training I learned how to crawl under barbed wire with an unloaded gun, and I met Yankees from all over the country.

I knew that these new skills, my uniform, and especially meeting Yankees from all over the country, would make me an extremely exotic-type person when I returned home on leave.

And here I was standing beside the road outside of Biloxi, hitchhiking on my first big trip ever. I was going to hitch all the way around the horn to McAllen.

I got a ride with an old gentleman in a beat-up old pick-up truck. He, his clothes, and the truck looked alike. Well-worn, old, clean, well-taken-care-of. An old gentleman, and I mean to tell you from the experiences of over twenty years of hitchhiking, this man was, in every sense of the word, a gentleman. He was an old black gentleman.

He liked me, and as we rolled along for a few miles he asked me real questions. Interesting questions, and I told him everything about the Rio Grande Valley, the river, the colors, the border, the people. I was like a young bird perched on the edge of that seat, chirping away about how I couldn't wait until I got home, couldn't wait until those guys back there saw me in this uniform. They would die of jealousy. "Funny," I said, "how I couldn't wait to get out of that place, and now I can't wait to get back." That made him sort of laugh. "Huh," he said.

I told him all about the trips I was going to take. I was going here, I was going there. That's why I joined the Air Force, to see the world. I was going to see the entire world. He liked it. He laughed. I remember at one point he looked over at me and said, "Oh, you're going to be a real pisser, ain't you, Jim?"

We laughed together.

We came to some road construction, and we were the only vehicle there. A man was standing in the road holding a *Stop* sign. A large black man in a prison uniform just outside Biloxi, Mississippi. As I looked past him, I saw seven or eight other men working very hard on the road with hand tools in the hot Mississippi afternoon sun. They were all in prison uniforms. All black men. I was looking at a road gang. I had never seen a road gang before.

Some movement I caught out of the corner of my eye turned my head off the road over into the shade of the trees, and there was the prison guard. He was a large man in a khaki prison uniform with a badge, a regular kind of Stetson style hat, no-see-through sun glasses and a thick black leather belt that held up a large silver-plated pistol, a blackjack, a pair of handcuffs, and a very healthy belly. He was holding a pump-action shotgun, and he had the stub of an unlit cigar in one corner of his mouth. He was a white man.

The man with the *Stop* sign stepped right up to the bumper of the truck, and when he did, he caught my eye and brought it back, and I looked at him. The first thing that struck me when

I saw him was, my God, this is the most beautiful person I have ever seen in my life. It is like looking at some kind of natural force, a waterfall or something. Man, woman, or child, this is the most beautiful person I have ever seen. And then I looked into his eyes. There was that freight train spotlight, that train light shining directly at me.

I could see clearly the force, the energy behind that spotlight. He hated me. And when I saw his face was full of hate, I do not mean that it was screwed up and twisted in some monstrous mask. Oh, no. His face was practically expressionless. It was the kind of look, the kind of expression, the kind of intensity you learn to be able to put into your eyes and into your face without changing anything on your face. It's a kind of skill. It's one of the skills you learn in prison.

He looked at me and he hated me. I knew people who told me they hated me. Hell, I'd been shot at, but it is like my brother Lorenzo told me once: "Hate is like the dark side of the moon, Jim." Well, I'm telling you that this hate had no back side. It was absolutely flat.

This was hate without a single question.

This was hate without a single doubt.

This was hate without a single expectation.

He turned and looked at the old black gentleman, and I knew the look would change. Maybe black to black, or maybe black to Uncle Tom, because the old gentleman was giving me a ride. it changed all right. The look. It changed to nothing. I don't mean to neutral. I mean nothing. He practically disappeared right before my eyes without even changing the expression on his face.

The guard blew his silver whistle and the black prisoner holding the *Stop* sign stepped aside, and we drove past him. I never saw him again.

We drove in silence. The old gentleman looked over at me. I was sitting there looking like I had just been run over by a train.

He said, "Don't take it so hard, Jim."

I said, "He hated me."

He said, "That's right, he did."

"Did they ever put you on a road gang like that?" I asked.

He laughed and spoke very quietly, very gently. "Hell, Jim, every black man my age around here has been on a road gang at one time or another, it seems like."

"I'm sorry," I said.

There was a short pause.

"What's that, Jim?"

I said, "I'm sorry."

"All right, yeah. Well, I guess that's all right, you being sorry and all, Jim. You listen to me, Jim. It ain't nearly enough."

"What do you mean?"

He said, "You take that guard. He's about as sorry as any human can be." And he laughed to himself. "Yes, sir, he's sorry, if you know what I mean. The point is, Jim, he's doing something on his side. He's out there working. You got to do at least as much on your side."

A pause, as we rattled and bumped down the highway in his old pick-up truck.

"Hell, Jim, on our side."

When he said that to me, I felt an instant of filling with pride.

Then he said, "Remember that place you told me you grew up?"

"Oh, yeah, the Rio Grande Valley."

"Yeah, that's it. What did you call those Mexicans who came illegally into Texas?"

"Oh," I said, "*Mojados*. Wet backs."

"That's right," he said. "I remember. And didn't they work around your houses as your maids or as your gardeners, or out in your fields, and out at the construction jobs? Weren't they working out in the sun?"

"Yeah," I said.

"Well, Jim, you say you never saw anybody look at you like that guy back there. You think about it. Maybe sometime you stepped out of the sun into the air-conditioned office, just because you are white. Maybe one or two of those *Mojados* looked at you like that, but you were so young, so full of yourself like we are when we are that age, and when they looked at you, you didn't even see it."

And I thought, he might be right. Might be right. Hell, he *is* right.

We came to a point in the road where he went one way and I went another. I jumped out and grabbed my duffle bag out of the back of the truck. It was huge. Must have weighed 80 pounds. It was full of my military and my civilian clothes. Everything I owned. One of those big, blue Air Force duffle bags with my name and serial number stenciled in white on the side.

He watched me struggle it up to my shoulder and leaned over to me and said, "Jim, you travel to this part of the country again and you ain't in uniform, you just take care, now here? They arresting white folks for nothing now, too." He started to chuckle to himself, and he said, "Jim, you going to be doing all that traveling you told me about?" He pointed at my pack. "You just got to learn to travel lighter than that." He laughed. "You take care now, hear." And he drove away.

I remember what it was like to look into his eyes. Oh, yes. His eyes were like a deep well. And when you drew the water from deep out of the earth, you just knew that that well water would taste cold and crisp and clean.

And then I remembered those eyes waiting for me out in front of the filling station. I remembered I hadn't been paying very close attention for the last few minutes, so I started to concentrate to see if the devil was sneaking up on me.

I said to myself, *He's probably gone by now. Probably gone. Are you crazy? The devil has infinite patience.* I continued talking to myself for a couple of minutes more, but I couldn't stand it in those tires any longer, so I crawled out as quietly as possible.

I crept around the back of the filling station and peeked out at the gas pumps and the driveway. Nothing. I poked my head out a little farther and looked around. The street was deserted. Nothing was moving. Not a single maroon Mercury in sight, but I was still scared, so I walked around the back of the filling station, past the tires on my left and then crawled out from behind the station, crawled up to the back corner of the large plate glass window that runs about two-thirds around the filling station office.

I peeked in the bottom corner of the window, and I could see the entire office. There's the filling station attendant with his feet on the desk and his nose glued to the *Playboy* magazine. It doesn't look like he has even turned the page. Nobody else. I watched the door to the men's room which was just behind the attendant. No one came out.

I'm still scared, so I sneak over to the door of the filling station, looking around all the time, and I very quietly open the door and the breeze comes in the door with me. The guy doesn't hear me but he feels the breeze, lowers the magazine and sees me

TRAVELING LIGHT

sneaking through the door. He throws the *Playboy* straight up in the air, screams, *aaaaahhhhhheeeeeee,* and falls backwards out of his chair.

You see, I'm covered in black slime from head to foot from the empty used tires, and I look like the creature from the Black Lagoon creeping through the front door to get him. I could see it flash across his face before he fell out of the chair: "I knew this would happen to me if I worked the midnight shift. I tried to tell them this would happen. *Aaaahhhhhh!*" He hit the floor crawling on all fours at top speed for the men's room.

Of course when he screamed and made a run for it, that scared the hell out of me, so I yelled and jumped and turned around and ran out the door, across the driveway and had to stop myself. *Stop, stop, Jim. What in the hell are you doing now?* I stopped running, turned around and walked back inside. He was peering out the restroom door.

"Oh my God," he said. "It's only you. Where in the hell have you been?"

"I was hiding out in those tires," I said.

"Our tires?" he asked. "What was you doing in them tires?" He wasn't afraid anymore. Now he was suspicious.

"I was hiding."

"Hiding? From who?"

I said, "Where's that old man?"

"What old man?"

"The one in the maroon Mercury?"

"Oh, him," he said. "He's long gone. Funny thing, now that I see you. I could have sworn there were two people in that car when he drove off. Yep, I could have sworn he gave you a ride out of here."

"Well, he didn't."

"What was you doing in them tires?"

I don't know what he thought I was going to with those empty used tires—put a couple on each arm like the Michelin man and run over Lookout Pass with them? I looked at him and I thought, can I tell this kid I was hiding in the bottom of a pile of used tires because I thought I was hiding from the devil, when I'm not even sure I can believe it myself?

I said, "It was a misunderstanding."

"Huh?" he said.

"I'll be right back," I said, and I went into the bathroom and cleaned up and changed clothes into the best and cleanest clothes I had, and when I came out I didn't look too good, but I didn't look like an escaped monster either, and his relief was there: Another young guy.

He said, "You scared the hell out of me. The least you can do is let me buy you breakfast." He was smiling. A really nice, pleasant face.

Travel tip number three. If at all humanly possible, never turn down a free meal.

We drove across Wallace in his new station wagon. It was only four or five blocks to the all-night diner, and along the way he pointed out several large two- or three-storey Victorian style houses, and a couple of them had neon signs. One said *Jane's Place* and another *Betty's*. When we passed the houses, he nudged me and said, "Those are the local sights. Ha, ha, ha."

"The what?" I asked.

"The local sights," and he laughed again. Not laughing like in a Charlie Chaplin movie, but sort of a conspiratorial laugh. He laughed again, and I thought, now I recognize that laugh. It is one of the good ol' boy kinds of laugh. "Those are the local sights," he said.

I said, "Are those whorehouses?"

He laughed. "I hope so. The local sights we call them," and he laughed again.

We went to breakfast. I ordered a huge meal. I never knew when I might eat again, so I always stocked up. The filling station attendant smiled at me when I ordered. He understood.

The local sheriff walked in, and that made me nervous. He sat with us, and that made me very nervous because I had learned right away as a little boy in McAllen, Texas, that the police have total discretionary powers, expecially over people who are rootless like hitchhikers. People like me. But he was a nice guy.

We had a couple of cups of coffee and then he stood up. He turned to the filling station attendant and said, "Don't let him leave town without seeing the local sights," and they all laughed, and then they looked at me, so I quickly joined in. He said again, "Don't leave town without seeing the local sights." We all laughed. The sheriff left. The filling station attendant paid our bill, shook my hand goodbye, and drove away.

I picked up my bag and hit the road. It was four or five blocks back to the filling station, which was the best place in town to hitch from. Walking down the street ahead I saw a neon sign flashing on and off: *Betty's, Betty's, Betty's.* I'm thinking as I walk towards the sign, "Gee, I've never been in an American whorehouse. I've been in a lot of Mexican ones, but never an American one. It would be sort of like scientific research."

A little closer. *Betty's, Betty's Betty's.* A two-tone sign, red and white. I think, "What the hell, it's late, very late, I'm tired. Maybe I could get a couple of hours of sleep and hit the road fresh with the dawn."

Betty's, Betty's, Betty's.

I stop in front of the house. The windows are closed and dark. *Who knows,* I said to myself. *Behind those dark windows may be fifteen or twenty men and women having a good time. Bands, music, dancing and drinking. Every sin the priest told me about could be happening right now right in there.*

Betty's, Betty's, Betty's.

Besides, I said to myself. *The sheriff told me not to leave town without seeing the local sights, and I wouldn't want to disobey the sheriff.* I walked up to the door and knocked. A tiny window slid open with a slap. It made me jump. I could see part of a face, an older woman with very red lips. She wanted to see my driver's license to make sure I was eighteen.

Right away, I see things are going to be different than in Mexico. I think, "Hell, I started going to whorehouses when I was thirteen years old. I wasn't big enough even to see over the wheel of a car, much less to have a driver's license." I showed her my driver's license and she let me in. I followed her up a steep stairway, dimly lit.

I said, "I'd like to stay all night."

"This ain't a hotel, honey."

We keep going up the stairs.

"I know," I said. "But I would like to stay the rest of the night with one of the girls."

"This ain't a hotel, honey."

We're at the top of the stairs.

"I know where I am," I said. "I would like to stay all night with one of the whores." She looked at me as if I just landed from another planet. "This ain't a hotel, honey."

I could see we weren't communicating. I said "OK, let's just have the daily special." She gave me that look again and took me into an empty room. I looked around. I said, "Where are the girls, where are the guys, where's the band, the whiskey, where are the good times?"

She said, "It's late."

I said, "I know, I know, so let's not waste any of my time. Let's get started."

She didn't think that was too funny.

She left me alone in the empty room and went to get one of "her girls." A sterile room. In Reynosa, all the rooms looked exactly alike. There was a bed, a shower, inside the shower a little douche, and a dresser with about a thousand religious artifacts. Even though every room was exactly alike, each room had its own distinct personality. But this room could have been a Holiday Inn room any place on the planet.

The madam brought in a nice-looking woman in her mid-twenties in a pair of dark panties. Madam left.

The lady in the panties said to me, "You can have this for that much and that for this much and this much for that." I had $50, so I did a little mental math and ended up having a little of this and a little of that.

As we lay down together, I remembered my ride across the desert and the sweaty dog and the stinking dead pigs. She was very professional and never blinked an eye. Before you know it, I was back out in the street again, right in front of the filling station.

It's still night; I still haven't gotten a ride out of Wallace, Idaho. I'm walking up and down by my bag talking to myself.

Jesus Christ, what was that all about? I might just as well have gone to a friendly doctor's office or something.

Another voice in my head said, *Oh, really, Jim, what's the matter? Don't you like it because it was such a straight business deal? Hasn't it always been a business deal?*

No, I said. *Not back in Reynosa. There was dancing, singing, good times. There it was more like being at a party where you always got laid.*

Oh, the voice said, *don't tell me you believed that shit the girls used to hand the tourists down from Amarillo. "I loofe ju, baby, I fuckie ju for free, but the room she cost cinco doughlers, cinco doughlers."*

No, no, no, I said. *I didn't believe that. I mean there was always money changed, but there was something else.*

Oh, really, what's the matter? Not enough fantasy in your life?
Oh, hell, I replied. *I don't know.*

A car was sitting in the street right in front of me. A ride. I was so involved in my conversation with myself, trying to figure out how I felt, that I didn't even see the car stop. I had no idea how long it had been sitting there. Who cares? I thought. A ride out of here at last. I jerked the door open and stopped. I looked very closely at the driver. A regular-looking guy, not the devil. I jumped in and we took off.

We quickly left the lights of Wallace behind. We started up toward Lookout Pass. We were on a mountain road winding up, up, up. It was pitch black. We talked a little. He asked where I was going, how long I had been waiting for a ride, the usual questions. I found out he was indeed a traveling salesman from Iowa. He had a wonderful voice. Sort of like an FM radio announcer's voice, smooth and mellow as it rolled out of the darkness into the car.

"It sure is black out there," he said.

"Certainly is," I said.

"Really black."

"You bet," I said.

"And deserted too," he said.

"Sure is," I said.

"Say," and his voice never changed inflection from the previous statements. "How would you like a good blow job?" he asked.

Aaahhhuuuggghhh. A siren went off inside my head. It struck me that in all my years in whoretown, I had never met a homosexual man. Not in Mexico, land of machismo. So what do I do now? A siren went off in my head again, *oommaahhoommhh.*

What to do when you meet a homosexual man!

The training from when I was a little boy all the way up until I graduated from high school, all the years hanging around places like the Rockin' Robin Drive Inn in McAllen, Texas, brought one central message screaming through my head at that moment, and that message had an actual physical imperative that went along with it. What to do when approached by a homosexual man?

Smash him!

Don't think about it. Don't think about it, because if you think about it, you might be thinking about It, and if you think about

It, that means you could be a latent homosexual. A closet queen, a disgusting fucking queer.

So what can you do to erase even the slightest doubt about your masculinity when approached by a homosexual man? Don't think about it.

Smash him.

Even to be asked as I was, suggested that the queer must have seen something latent in you that only queers can see, so how did I erase even the slightest doubt about that question?

Smash him.

And I was about to do just that. My arm was coming up when another siren went off in my head, followed closely by a voice that was very clear and very fast. *Stop, stop, stop! You are on a mountain road, and if you hit him in the head, he will drive off the road and we will both go over a cliff, and we will both be killed. Stop, stop, stop! Don't hit him.*

And then I heard a third voice. A voice I had never heard in my head before. It was a little child's voice in an empty building. This voice said, *Why don't you just listen to what he is saying? Don't be afraid; he's not threatening you.*

Mmmeeegggaaammmeeegggaaa threat! threat! Of course it's a threat! What if he has a gun, a knife, a hidden partner?

Smash him.

And his voice was rolling on. "Have you ever really had a good one?"

"What, what?" I said.

"Oh, no," I think to myself, "I've got to get myself under control and talk to this guy."

"A really good blow job?" he asked. "Did you ever have one?"

And I said, "Oh, ah, gee, no. I mean, I don't know. I was just in this place in Wallace, and she, no, no, I mean, that's not what we are going to talk about."

I could see all the faces from the Rio Grande Valley yelling at me, telling me what to do, judging me, and these faces were rushing by like a waterfall, when I suddenly realized that they were not in the car with me at this moment. They were not anywhere to be seen. I was in this car on the side of the mountain all by myself. Hell, I thought, when I left the Rio Grande Valley I was glad to leave it behind. Those people don't have anything to do with my life anymore. I don't have any past. What those people thought

TRAVELING LIGHT

was cool or right doesn't make any difference to me any more, and if I wanted to let this guy give me a blow job, it was none of their goddamn business. It was my business, period. I didn't have any past any more, and as I realized that, I felt like someone had cut all the cords that had been holding me to the earth, and I started to float around inside the car. My stomach actually felt queasy, like I was on a carnival ride.

I didn't have any roots any more, so I was floating around, lost, and at that moment the child's voice said, *Wait a minute, Jim. All you have got to do is be able to look yourself in the eye in the mirror in the morning.* I remembered that when I was a little boy, my two older brothers always washed their faces in the morning, and I would yell, "me, me" and one of them would pick me up to the sink so that I could wash my face and then stand me on the sink so I could look in the mirror and look myself in the eye, and I have been doing it every morning ever since. That child's voice was cutting through the bad shit.

Just make sure you can look yourself in the eye in the mirror in the morning, Jim. Right, right, right. I realized I had to set my own course here. I had to get myself under control, get on top of it. I took a deep breath. I thought, if I want to let him, I'll let him, and if I don't I won't, and I don't, so I won't, and that's it.

I turned to him, and I said in a voice that matched his for coolness and mellowness, "No, thank you."

Just like that I said, "No, thank you."

I did not scream and thrash around like a berserker yelling, "Don't touch me, don't touch me."

"No," I said, "No, thank you."

He asked, "Are you sure? Have you ever really had a good blow job?"

"No, I'm simply not interested."

But I thought to myself, I'm really on top of it now. We are two adults having a conversation.

"Really, wouldn't you?"

"No," I cut him off. "No, thank you."

"I could pull over."

"Don't. Don't pull over." My radiator was beginning to boil again.

"There is a place up here."

"Don't do anything. Don't try to rape me?"

"What!" he yelled, "Rape you?"

"Don't try it, Mister."

"What are you talking about? I'm not going to try anything."

"Don't try anything, because if you do, I'll smash your fuck-ing brains out. I'm a bad mother-fucker, and I don't care if I die."

"Please don't hit me," he said. "I don't know what you are talking about. I'm not going to try anything."

"Oh yeah, just don't," I screamed, holding up my fist in a threatening gesture. He shrank against his door.

Silence. We drove up the side of the mountain into the black night. Clouds cut off the moon and the forest grew tall on both sides of the highway and made the road look like a tunnel.

I was thinking to myself, "Well, Jim, you just found out some-thing about being 'on top of it'; sometimes it doesn't last very long."

I was sitting pressed against my door ready to spring out. I was sitting very still and not thrashing around, but inside I was on an emotional roller coaster. I was afraid. What if he's got a knife, a gun, a partner? What do I do out here all by myself on the side of this mountain? I was frustrated. What am I supposed to do— hit him? Do nothing? Frustration changed into fear, into anger, but the voice was saying, *No, no, don't hit him. Not while he's driv-ing.* And the child's voice saying, *Just relax Jim, just relax.* Up and down I went.

I looked over at him. Just for a moment I could actually get out of myself and see him. I thought, my God, he's just a guy. He's just sitting there driving along, looking very calm like me but, I thought, I bet he's going crazy inside, too. I mean, he picked me up, a complete stranger. He doesn't know what kind of a per-son I am. He doesn't know what I might be carrying.

I was looking at him, and at that moment we pulled into a little all-night diner. It was very close to Lookout Pass, very close to the Pass. I was still in Idaho, a long way from Superior, Mon-tana, where he told me he was going. The diner was in the mid-dle of a very big nowhere.

I said, "What in the hell is this? I thought you were going to Superior, Montana?"

"I'm turning around here and going back to Wallace."

"What? What do you mean, you're going back?"

"I'm going back to Wallace."

"You can't let me out here. I would never have gotten in the car if I had known you were going to do this."

He said, "Please, please, you frighten me."

"I frighten you? That's rich."

"Please don't be angry."

I got out.

And I am even more confused now, and I am pissed off. I'm up at about 8,000 or 9,000 feet now, and it is freezing ass. There is no light on the road, so I will never get a ride. I am stuck here for the rest of the night and probably longer. I still didn't know what I was supposed to have done, and he is pulling away. My emotions boil over; I kicked the hell out of his back fender. *Aaaahhhhhoooo, wham.*

As soon as I kicked his car, I felt stupid. I felt silly, bad silly, like I had been dipped in ice cold, filthy water.

It didn't do my hitchhiking much good, either. Just as I kicked the car, two young guys, the kind of guys who would give me a ride, stepped out of the diner, and saw me kick the car and one of them said, "What was that all about?"

Kicking the car was pretty bad, but at least at that moment I did not say, "Oh, he's some faggot trying to get hold of me, but I kicked his car, good manly thing to do, so you can give me a ride, because I proved I'm a regular guy."

I didn't say that. All I said was, "We had a misunderstanding. Which way are you guys headed?"

"Which way you headed?" one of them asked.

Oh, oh, I think. "Montana," I say.

"Too bad," one of them says. "We're going to Idaho." They got in their car and drove about thirty feet into Idaho, turned around and *vvvvoooooommmmm* right by me, toward Montana.

I shot them the finger will full arm extension and yelled, "Adios, pende-jos."

I heard this laughing behind me. I turned around and an old drunk has come out of the diner. He was carrying two six packs of beer and wearing a greasy baseball cap that said LA Dodgers. He was laughing at me. He said, "I've never seen anyone hitchhike like that before. I like it. Where you going, kid?"

"Montana," I said.

"Montana," he said, like it was Timbuctoo. "Yeah, sure, I'll go there. Come along, kid."

We got in his car and took off. Quickly we were up and over the Pass and on our way down the other side. We were screaming and screeching around the corners. He looked at me and said, "You don't mind, I say, kid, I hope you don't mind if I cut the corners a little bit, do yuh?" And we went around the corner *rrrrruuuuurrrrrrmmmmm*. "I'm on my toot," he said.

"Your what?" I asked?

"My toot, toot. I'm drunk. I do this every four or five months. *Eeeerrrreeeeemmmmmmrrrrr*."

"I've been traveling over these roads all my life. Say kid, how would you like a beer? *Eeeerrrroooooeeeee*."

I said, "I'd love a beer."

And by the time we reached the bottom of the mountain, we'd drunk both of those six packs and were well on our way through a third. We came screeching to a halt.

"That's my friend's place, kid."

I saw a small motel, grocery store and filling station, all closed and dark.

"Looks closed to me."

"It is," he said. "But he'll let me in."

I got out.

"See you around, kid."

He disappeared around the back of the buildings.

I was standing beside the highway and the sun was starting to rise. The Rocky Mountains' eastern slope was lit up by the rising sun. I could see that the road ran through a pine forest. The sunlight brought the forest to life. The birds were starting to wake up. I saw them flying between the green pine trees, and their wings flashing their colors were like welcoming smiles. On the other side of the road, I saw a small stream just bubbling and dancing along. I smelled the dawn air.

Oh, yeah, I said. I'm going to get a ride here any minute. I'm hot, hot, hot. Just got a ride here, didn't I? All right, all right, the sun is coming up, and that means that people who work on the earth will be on the road, yeah, lumber trucks, lumberjacks, oil field workers, farmers, ranchers, anybody who works with the rhythm of nature. They will give me a ride. Maybe a semi-trailer truck. A traveling salesman. The early worm gets the sale. They all hit the road right about now, so I'm going to get a ride real quick. I'll be home in Great Falls, Montana, by this afternoon. Yeah, and as soon as I get back to Great Falls, I'm going to take a shower. I haven't had a shower for days. And I am going to shave.

I think about that. *Oh, Jim,* I said to myself, *I bet when you get back and you look in that mirror to shave, and you look yourself in the eye, the face you see in there looking back out at you, it's going to be a little bit different now, isn't it?*

Oh, yeah.

You're going to see some new lines on that face, deep one here, a couple more over there, oh yeah, and you will say to yourself, "Wallace, Idaho, a hell of a town."

Esta Es Mi Llave

I am riding in the back seat of a Chevy being driven by one of my oldest friends in the world. His name is Eddie. We have known each other all our lives. We grew up in the same neighborhood in McAllen, Texas. His wife, Bianca, was riding shotgun. A beautiful woman. Quite stunning. Her mother was Mexican, and from her she inherited a golden brown skin. Her father was an Irish Texan, and from him she inherited blonde hair, with a touch of red, which fell to her waist. In Spanish, her hair was called "Colorado." She was five foot ten, and she looked as if she was born to wear Levis and cowboy shirts.

The three of us are on vacation together. I hadn't seen Eddie in a couple of years, but when we met again it was as if the conversation just dovetailed into mid-sentence of where we left off years before. After a couple of days in McAllen, we had been talking, drinking, driving around and seeing the sights, and I said that I would like to get into Mexico, into the interior. Eddie said, "Hell fire, Jim, let's go." Eddie had a job that made it possible for him to leave town at a moment's notice. Indeed, Eddie had a job where it was imperative that he be able to leave town at a moment's notice. So the three of us jumped into his new Chevy and took off to Mexico, looking for the Hotel Buena Vista.

A friend of Eddie's, a contact, he called him, described the hotel to us in one of those high-pitched Texas drawls. "Sheiitt Eddie, it's jest in-cred-e-bull. Way up in the mountanes. See, thar wuz spposed to be this here huuge dee-vel-o-ment 'cept nothin' got built 'cept this hoetel," he cackled. "It's thrae stories tall, thrae rest-two-rants and thrae bars and thrae swimmin' pools. Hell fire, Eddie, you kud all switch pools and rums ever nat. Noobody ever *stays* thar. They practicly pay yew ta stay ther. Thay got horsy-back ridin', and a lit o' bit of a lake rat ther'. It's dirt cheap, hell boy, it's par-a-dace."

So we are looking for "par-a-dace," driving through the mountains of Mexico at night, lost. If this was a photograph with the headline "What's wrong with this picture?" you could draw a lot of circles around the wanderings.

We finally came upon a small mountain village. When we get to the edge of the village, I see, in the headlights, three men walking out of the village. The man in front is wearing the white cotton pants worn by the *campesinos* all over Mexico. He is shirtless, wearing General Popo sandals, which are sandals made with a little leather and part of the tread of a General Popo tire for the sole of the sandal. His hands are tied behind his back, and he has a white bandage tied around his chest with a bright stripe of blood through it. Walking right behind him are two of what we call in Mexico the "blue meanies," police with blue shirts, blue helmets, blue pants, black-blue boots, and brand new blue-black machine guns. They disappear into a hole cut into the jungle wall. A doorway into another world.

During the day, when we were driving through the mountains and I looked across the jungle, I couldn't see a single sign of life, though I know that it is teeming with life. Seen from above the canyon, the canopy of trees is so complete that all I can see is an unbroken sea of green. The jungle grows straight up beside the road. There are walls of orchids. I cannot see one inch inside. Then I see one of those little doors. A hole cut about five feet tall. Over the years, I have seen people pop in and out of those doors and wondered where they came from and where they went. I know that stepping into one of those jungle doors would transport me into a world as fantastic as any Alice ever saw.

The men disappeared into the jungle doorway, and I say "Gee, that's odd. They're taking that guy away from town." Bianca looks at me and smiles. Eddie laughs. "You have been livin' with the Yankees too long, Jim. This is the mountains of Mexico, remember?"

"Oh yah," I thought. Some summary justice is about to be carried out. The blue meanies would report back to their commander later that the prisoner tried to escape, so they had been forced to shoot him.

The village is closed down tight for the night, but in the cantina we find an old man with a huge Zapata mustache who says he knows where the Hotel Buena Vista is. He speaks no English and Eddie and I speak only clumsy Spanish. Bianca speaks fluent Spanish, so she does all our complex Spanish speaking for us, but the mustache is old-fashioned, so he won't talk to Bianca because she is a woman. Instead, he looks at Eddie and he acts like Eddie is talking as Bianca speaks. Then he speaks directly to Eddie to answer him. Bianca translates for us as Eddie looks at the old man. The old mustache looks at Eddie. As I sat outside the triangle, I felt I was watching a sort of three-way ventriloquist act.

We drive out of town, following his instructions. We find a red bandana tied to a tree limb on the left-hand side of the road. We take the next road to the left. That road is supposed to be one mile from the Hotel. The road is still climbing up the mountain, and the two-lane blacktop has quickly become a one-lane gravel road. In some places I have to get out of the car and walk up the road to see if we can make it. It took us an hour to go that mile.

We finally round a corner and there it is, the Hotel Buena Vista: three stories tall with wrought-iron balconies, French windows, forty or fifty rooms, and every one of them facing the view. In the moonlight, you can see for miles across the mountain ranges, one peak after another floating in the clouds and fog and mist. We look down into the canyon and there is a small lake like a dark jewel, gleaming. In the daylight the view must be fantastic.

Silence. The sound of the car engine idling. We look closer, and in the headlights, we can see that some of the trees by the front of the Hotel have grown onto the balconies and have taken over the front of the place. The jungle vegetation has also grown down over part of the roof onto the balconies and is headed for the double French doors. Every room was dark. The Hotel Buena Vista is a portrait in blackness: The jungle surrounding us, the black mountain ranges and peaks, the black jewel lake, and three storeys of black rooms. Blackness, except for one dim light in one corner of the hotel.

We've got to admit to each other that we are pretty Goddamn spooked by this place. Who's going in, we ask each other? Bianca says, "Look guys, is this an adventure or what?"

"Well, yes," we say.

"All right then," she says. "I speak the best Spanish, so I'll go in."

Eddie and I finally agree to that. Now, we ask, who will stay with the car? Just because we can't see anyone doesn't mean that there is no one out there. We all know more about Mexico than that. I say, "Eddie, you are the best driver by far, and if we have to leave in a hurry, I would feel much better if you were behind the wheel." Eddie asked Bianca what she thought about that. She laughed. "Oh yeah," she said. "I guess old Jim and I can handle it, whatever it might be. Come on, Jim."

Bianca and I walked through the headlights towards the front door, across a huge patio of red tile and brick. On this patio at one time, the restaurant must have put out tables with white linen table clothes, china, cut glass, and heavy, real silverware. Waiters with towels over their arms in white-coated tuxedos would have served mangos, papaya, fresh bread, pouring hot cups of coffee from a solid silver coffee pot. Now there were just a few tables and chairs tipped over and scattered about, and in the shadows they looked like the skeletons of prehistoric animals.

Bianca and I walked up to the front doors. They are twelve feet high, solid oak with ornate carving all the way around the edge. Imitations of Mayan and Aztec carvings. People's hearts being ripped out on top of a pyramid and things like that. The door handles are huge bird heads, and I have to reach down inside their beaks to grasp the door handles.

I pull the door open and the hinges scream and screech like the door on the old radio program, "Inner Sanctum." We can see into a lobby three storeys tall in the center, rising to a skylight that is broken out now. The ornate rug is torn and stained. There are writing desks, sofas, chairs and stand-up ashtrays, all broken and scattered around the room. The check-in desk of teak with the key holds a wall of tiny, dark, empty spaces, miniatures of the rooms in the hotel. The lobby is lit by one uncovered light bulb hanging in the center of the room from a series of extension cords that snake out of sight up towards the third floor somewhere. The light hangs at about the height where it would be easy for someone about 5'6" to turn it on and off. Three hallways led off into different directions; we could see a little way down the halls until they became dark, darker, then pitch black. When we opened the door, the breeze started the light bulb swinging around on the end of that three-storey-long extension cord, and the shadows began to dance around inside the lobby like the inside of a swimming pool. Standing in the doorway taking it all in, holding hands, we must have looked a little like Hansel and Gretel.

Bang! the door opens on the far left of the lobby, and the light spills into the lobby. The caretaker is standing silhouetted in the doorway, a short heavy-set man, five foot six or so, 190 pounds, no shirt, white pants and the General Popo sandals. The smell of cheap tequila spreads across the lobby. Sweat rolls down his body.

"*Buenas noches, amigos.*" He waves his arms in a grand gesture and almost falls down. He laughed with his mouth wide open, the laugh exploding out of his belly, a laugh with no humor in it at all.

"*Bien venidos, amigos.* Welcome to Hotel Buena Vista. Are ju lookin' for a room? No, no, no," he went on. "Ju gringos always say," he held up his hands with palms up, "*Hay cuantos aqui,*" he laughed again rocking back and forth in the doorway and he repeated much louder. "*Hay cuantos aqui.*" He did a perfect imitation of an American speaking bad Spanish, and then his face changed and he asked, "Do either of you speak any Spanish?"

Bianca stepped into the lobby and walked towards him. I followed. He could see Bianca clearly now and his mouth fell open. He could see her white hair, haloed by the light bulb. She was at least four or five inches taller than he. You could see him thinking: *at last; it has finally happened. The Nordic Goddess from the land of ice where it is always cool, she has come to deliver me from this stinking, rotting, sweaty, black purgatory.*

Bianca spoke to him in perfect Spanish. "We would like to see a room, please? It was a long day and we are tired. We would like to see a room, please."

His face went through a series of wild contortions. His Goddess had spoken, but she had asked for a room. "What, *que? que?*" thinking, *this is not what is supposed to happen.* Then he saw me for the first time. "What?" he said out loud. "*Que*, see room. Are ju serious?" and he swept his arms around to show us the place, just in case we were serious.

Bianca was undaunted by him. She was used to men being sort of thunderstruck when they first met her, especially Latin American men. She pushed ahead. "Of course we are serious. We would like to see a room please?"

"Is he," he asked, pointing at me, "your husband?"

We looked at each other and both understood that a long explanation would not be a good idea. She said "yes, *si, si, si*. A room."

Then he began to repeat after her, "*Si, si, si*. A room?" Then he laughed again. "You bet, I'll show you a room, *un momentito.*"He rolled around and disappeared into his room. I noticed he moved very lightly on his feet for a short, fat drunk guy.

I said "Bianca, shit, I don't know. This guy is pretty screwed up. Maybe we should get the hell out of here."

She laughed. "So he looks a little drunk to you, huh. Well, so would you be, if you had his job. He looks like your kind of guy to me. You and Eddie and him. You all like tequila. Maybe he'll give you guys a shot or two. Relax."

The caretaker came lurching back, and in one hand he was holding a large silver flashlight, the kind you can stand on the floor, and several room keys. All that in one hand, because in the other hand he was holding a machete. He saw me looking at the machete and laughed. "Don't worry, *viejito*, little husband," he says. "This *cucharo*." I think to myself—knife! "Is for *ratones*," he says.

Rats. I do not want to meet a rat that big, and I am not sure I can believe him, but it is better than any of the alternatives I can think of.

He takes off across the lobby towards one of the black hallways. We follow, keeping our distance from the machete which he is waving around as he lurches and reels across the lobby. I look around and I am wondering how all the rooms can be facing one side when the hallways lead off in three directions.

He crosses to the first door in the closest hall. He is muttering under his breath a rich refrain of Spanish curses. At the door, he sets down the flashlight. Its beam shoots straight up, lighting him from below. He tries to get one of the keys to work, metal scraping as he misses the lock. He jiggles it, curses, rattles the door handle. He whirls and throws the key down the hallway into the darkness.

I can hear it go bing, ping, and then he smiles at us. That sight spooked me worse than anything I had seen so far. "*Un momentito*," he said. "What you would call a Mexican minute, humm?" And he turned and tried another key. It didn't work. He tried another. He grew angrier and angrier. The curses grew louder and louder. He tried another key and then spun and threw all the keys into the darkness, bing, ping, ding.

All I could hear was his breathing. And I noticed that I was pouring sweat and the lobby looked about a hundred yards all the way across to the front door.

He laughed and held up the machete. "*Esta es la llave*." He waved it above his head, and, with a powerful stroke, smashed it into the lock of the door. The door handle flew off and down the hall after the keys. The door burst open, *wham*, and the flashlight spills into the room. I see a couple of beds, a table, chairs, rug, top quality stuff, but it all looks bad now. The furniture, I notice, is that phony Spanish kind with the heavy round-shaped legs; in the shadows, all the furniture looks like it is made from the Michelin Man.

"*Esta es la llave!*" he yelled and turned and backhanded the door across the hall. That door handle flew to join the rest of the hotel parts. The door banged open. He reeled down the hall to the next door. "*Esta es la llave,*" he screamed. Smash. The door handle flies off and the door bangs open. "*Esta es la llave.*" Another back hander. Another door handle, and this time the door comes off its hinges and crashes into the room raising a cloud of dust that covers him.

He reels towards us, the machete gleaming and flashing in the light. "*Esta es la llave.*" He comes to a stop right in front of us. The sweat cuts through in rivulets through the covering of grime and dust. He rocks back and forth. He focuses his eyes on Bianca, on his face a mix of hopelessness and dreams. "Colorado! Colorado!" he says. Bianca doesn't move. She looks back at him. He turned and looked right over the tip of the machete. He was holding it waist-high, point up. He knew how to handle that thing. He probably spent more time as a kid with one of those in his hands than I did with a baseball bat in mine. A working tool. He was looking at me over the tip like a snake looks at a mouse.

My brain is stripping its gears, because I can guess what he might open next with his key. Then I say from nowhere, "I love this room. Oh yes, I love this room. We'll take it."

Bianca picks up on this right away and starts to translate. He can't believe his ears and starts to howl with laughter. "Ju like this room?" More laughter. "Ju like this room?" he asked in English.

"Oh, yes, I love it," I say. "We'll take it." I take hold of Bianca's arm and we start to slowly back away. Nice and easy. We didn't want to set off any pursuit impulses.

He was staggering towards us. "Ju like this room?" He laughed again. The machete was waving around. We kept on slowly backing across the lobby that looked about two football fields across right about now.

"Ju want this room?"

"Oh, yes," Bianca said. "We think it's charming." The word charming brought me to a stop.

"Wait right there," she said to him. "We have to get our money. We'll be right back." She tugged on my arm and got me going again. "Wait," she said.

"Wait," he said.

"We'll be right back," Bianca said, flashing him a big beauty contest winner's smile. He just kept coming. He could sense things were slipping away from him.

"You wait," he yelled in Spanish.

"In fact, we like the room so much we'll take the other rooms too. Yep, we like all the rooms, we'll take them all. Two rooms, three rooms," I said.

"*Que?*" he yelled. "*Que?* You want two rooms, three rooms?" That stopped him. We kept right on heading for the door. "Two rooms," he laughed so hard he almost fell down, and he started after us again.

"Oh yes," Bianca said. "We will need rooms for our friends who have been hunting." We are backing a little faster but are still trying to look casual. "Hunting," she yelled at him. She said, "Hunting with friends. We've got lots of guns."

"Guns?" he said. That stopped him.

"Oh yes," Bianca said, "we have lots of guns, pistols, rifles, shotguns, machine guns, the works."

"Machine guns? You got no machine guns. I saw ju drive up. Ju got no guns. I sawed ju." He started to lurch towards us. Bianca and I looked at each other and thought, what the hell, and took off running toward the door.

We ran out the front door, and we could hear him yelling behind us. "*Alto, alto, Colorado,* wait! *Alto!*"

We ran across the patio and there was the car already turned around with the doors open. We leaped into the car and we roared away, the doors slamming. Eddie looked over at me and asked very casually, "We are leaving, right?" He's made this sort of exit before.

I looked back as we were pulling away, and I see the little man in the doorway with the machete waving and gleaming, and he was yelling, "*Colorado,* wait for me, *Colorado,* wait for me, please, wait for me, *Coloradooooooo!*"

Turning Forty

I am on a deserted beach outside a small fishing village on the Pacific Coast of Central Mexico at night in the full moonlight. Running beside me is the woman I love, and her long hair is blowing in the Pacific breeze like a dark flag. We are running easy and relaxed, just starting to break a sweat. Ahead of me for as far as I can see is deserted beach and ridge after dark ridge of the Sierra Madre Mountains, running in broken lines right into the Pacific Ocean. Those ridges are illuminated now only in spots by the moonlight, and I know that those mountains are covered in impenetrable jungle.

To my left, running parallel to the beach, is a coconut grove, a coconut forest. The floor of the grove is open, so I can see the moonlight dancing on the coconut forest floor and the palm fronds waving in the breeze.

We run in and out of the breaking waves. I look into the coconut forest, and I can see each coconut trunk curving up as graceful as the backbone of a ballerina. Then I see some life in the back of the grove. Whatever it is, it is huge, charging through the shadows. I can't make out the shape. It constantly changes shape. It's brown, white, black, red, golden and blue. Blue? Blue! A horse's eye. Fourteen or fifteen wild horses explode out of the coconut grove onto the beach, race across the sand in front of us and charge into the surf.

They turn and run up the beach away from us, bucking, kicking, biting and frolicking in the warm Pacific surf in the full moonlight. The woman I love and I are chasing after them, falling further and further behind. That's all right. We feel grand. I'm turning forty, the evening of my fortieth birthday.

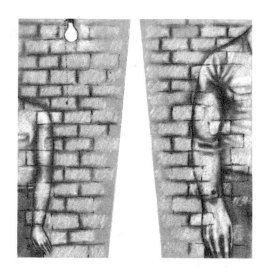

Raymond and Raymond

I am getting into the back seat of a new Ford Fairlane. My bag is thrown in and the door is closed behind me. I am struck immediately by a powerful, pungent, bitter smell, and then the overlay of a strong ammonia-based cleanser. It is clear to me that someone has thrown up in this backseat, and quite recently, too. But I think, at least they cleaned it up. There are no handles for the windows or the doors.

I am just outside Kansas City headed north. I am hitchhiking, headed for Great Falls, Montana, where I am stationed in the United States Air Force. I am on leave and I am in uniform. I left McAllen, Texas, two days ago where I had gone to my brother Jerry's wedding. My parents, who had moved to Florida and started a business, couldn't make it because of the time and money involved and because they couldn't travel the way I could: Hitchhiking from Great Falls to McAllen in four-and-a-half days without a penny in my pocket. Being in uniform helped a lot.

I managed to make it a few days before the wedding. Jerry had driven down from Austin, Texas, where he had just graduated from the University of Texas. My brother Lorenzo was living in the old family home which my parents were trying, with very little luck, to sell. There was no electricity, but there was water. Who needed electricity?

During the day, Jerry would go off on his wedding duties, and Lorenzo and I would climb into his two-tone green and white Ford Galaxy, drive to the 7-Eleven, buy some ice for our little ice box, a couple of six packs of Lone Star long necks and a box of .22 caliber shells, .22 shorts.

We'd cruise out onto the country road at a leisurely pace, open a couple of beers, turn on the radio, talk to each other, and watch for white-winged doves sitting on a telephone line. When we saw some, Lorenzo would glide the car to a stop. I would slide out the door, pull out that loaded .22 and, *pufft*, I would pick off one of those doves. The others would take off. I'd run over, and, with my trusty Boy Scout knife, clean that bird up and throw it in the ice box, and we would cruise again. We'd crack open another beer and talk about women and football and life. We'd stop, and *pufft*, another bird. That .22 short bullet made a tiny sound. Hell, you could clear your throat louder than that. But we didn't need to worry. There was very little traffic on those back dirt roads. Maybe farmers, oil or gas field workers. And as we were driving around, we might see some fresh corn and green peppers and tomatoes, oranges and watermelon.

We'd arrive home in the evening with a full ice box, and then sit out on the old family patio and barbeque those birds and corn, slice open those tomatoes, eat like royalty, drink a few beers, gaze up at the stars and talk, talk, talk. A rich time for the three brothers to meet as adults for the first time in their lives.

On a sunny day, Jerry got married to a wonderful woman, and, since my leave was almost up, I said good bye to my brother Lorenzo, and put my thumb out on Highway 281 headed north to Kansas City, where there was a huge Air Base with planes coming and going from the Air Force, the Army, the Navy, civilian, semi-civilian, everybody all over the country and the world. I was going to catch a hop.

Catching a hop is simple. You are on leave, in uniform, or on what is called TDY, temporary duty. You go down to the air strip on the base, find the right sergeant, the one who has the list of where everybody is going, get the OK. from the sergeant and the pilot of the plane, and usually you can jump on and take off. There was a lot of traffic between my station in Montana and the base in Kansas City. I figured that if I got a hop in Kansas City, it could save me two or three days of hungry, cold hitchhiking. It seemed like a good idea at the time.

I got a ride with a guy in Wichita. We hit it off right away, so when we got to Kansas City, he gave me a ride out to the base, ten or fifteen miles outside of town. At the main gate is a guard kiosk, the kind where the guard can lean out and check traffic coming and going. There is a small police station off to the side of the road, just inside the gate, to handle administrative duties.

It was late at night when we came out of the countryside darkness into the bright lights of the main gate of the Air Base. There was one policeman in the kiosk, an older sergeant. He leaned into the car and looked at me. I handed him my leave papers and explained that I am there to catch a hop. He looked at my leave papers and then back at me. Then he went back into the kiosk and studied my papers.

"Why did he take your papers?" the driver asked.

"Probably ashamed to have you discover that he can't read without moving his lips," I said. We laughed. The cop picked up his two-way radio, and I could see that he was talking to the police inside the office.

"Why is he doing that?" the driver asked.

"Relax," I said. "He's probably having them explain the big words to him." We sort of laughed, but I wondered myself why he was doing that.

Then the policeman came out of the kiosk, leaned in the driver's window and said to me: "Aer man Stol' wood yew step in cher, please." He turned and went back into the guard kiosk.

"Is there something the matter?" the driver asked.

"Oh no," I said. "S.O.P. Standard Operating Procedure. These guys just like to throw their weight around a little. They have all seen too many John Wayne movies. I'll be right back."

As I was getting out of the car, I am wondering what the hell was going on. Inside the kiosk, the sergeant who had been studying my papers took a good look at me. I look back. He is what is known as a "lifer," someone who will be in the service for the rest of his life. Some sign on and some are just born to it. Being known as a lifer is either an insult or a compliment, depending on who you talk to. This sergeant was one of those Southerners I had met in the service who came from a place so poor that life in the military looked like life with the Rockefellers.

He said, "Yew look like sheet."

Well, I didn't have on my hat and I did need a shave and a haircut and I did look like I had been sleeping in my uniform for a couple of days. I had. And I didn't have on exactly regulation shoes. Well, they were black and had the right number of eye holes but they had high, wooden heels. Those shoes drove the officers back where I was stationed crazy.

"Yeah, sure, Sarge," I said. "But I am on leave, so give me a fuckin' break. I'm just here looking for a hop." I was starting to get mad. I said, "You don't like my looks. Fine. I'll get back in the car and get out of your life." I turned to leave.

"Stop, Aer man Stol'. Halt." Now I knew something was wrong, but I didn't know what. The air policeman said "And what daay ar' yew dew bak at yur station?"

"What? Oh," I said. "You mean when is my leave over? The 28th."

"And what is t'daay's dayt?"

At that moment one of the other guards from across the road stepped into the kiosk. It was getting crowded in there, and when he stepped inside, he didn't give me a big smile and wave and say, "hi," or anything like that.

"What?" I asked.

"What is t'daay's dayt?" As he got more pissed off, his accent got thicker.

"Today's date. Hell I don't know. General LeMay's birthday?"

"What is t'daay's dayt?"

"Oh. What is today?" It seemed to me I spent a lot of time in the service translating lifer-speak into English.

"Today is the 26th," I said.

Pause. The two policemen looked at each other. I had seen that look before, and I felt something cold in my lower belly.

The sergeant pointed at the calendar. "Todaay's daayte is the 30th. Yew ar' tew daays laate. Tew daays AWOL. Absent without leave."

"Wait a minute," I said. "Wait a minute. I work with Control Data computers. I'm a computer operator. I don't even work with the Air Force. I work with the people with brains."

At that moment a squad car pulled up to the kiosk.

"I'm not even in the Air Force, practically speaking. I work with Control Data every day. I'm an unofficial Control Data employee, and you can't be AWOL from Control Data. I'm just two days late for work."

The guard looked at me. Flat, stone eyes. "Yew'r in the Yew Ninted States Air Foorse. Yew'r tew daays AWOL. Yew'r under a'rest, smart ass."

He turned and explained to the guy driving the car who kept looking at me with his eyes growing wide. As he drove away, I saw him glance at me. I could see on his face he felt he had narrowly escaped from Jack the Ripper. *Wheeyouu,* he was probably saying, I got away from that guy just in the nick of time.

Then they put me in the backseat of the new Ford Fairlane and I could smell the vomit and the cleanser. We're headed for the base stockade, and I was thinking that there was going to be one very happy Colonel back in Great Falls, Montana.

You see, I didn't adjust to life in the military very well. I've got to admit a lot of it was my own fault. I would get promoted because I was good at my job, and then do something like show up drunk, two hours late for work on the midnight shift of watching our radar sets waiting for the Great Russian invasion from the skies. I would cheerfully admit everything the next morning at my hearing. They always liked my honesty and then busted me.

Zip, off would go my stripe. I would do my job so well that I would earn my stripe back, and then I would say something, like the time I told my commander on the midnight shift that, since we both knew we really disliked each other, why didn't we just come out and admit it, and then he could get me transferred off his shift. I pointed out that it was a well-known fact that we hated each other. So I got busted for admitting that I disliked an officer. I was one of those guys they said had zippers on their stripes. Zip on, zip off, on, off, on, off.

When my brother's wedding came up, I applied for my leave. I had been saving up my leave time for a year, but because of my past record, my commander laughed when I asked him.

"Is this wedding really important to you, Stowell?"

"Yes, sir, my brother and I are very close."

The idea of some member of the human race being close to me seemed to amaze him. Then he laughed.

"You are a real pain in the ass, you know that, Stowell? No way, Jose. Leave denied due to personnel shortage. Sound good enough for you, you little son-of-a-bitch, now get the fuck out of my office."

I exercised my rights and went above his head to his commander. I broke the "chain of command," and that, of course, finished me off forever with my commander, but I figured after our little talk I didn't seem to have a whole helluva lot to lose.

I stood in that commander's office, which was larger than my commander's office, and he read my leave request and my commander's negative recommendation, which meant that in order for him to approve my leave, he would have to overrule his own officer in favor of an enlisted man.

He said, "I see here that they are short of personnel in your department. Leave denied, Airman Stowell, due to personnel reasons."

"Yes, sir, I understand, sir, but I am exercising my right and going over your head."

"What!"

And I did, and of course that buried me a little deeper. I kept going deeper until I went all the way to the top. To the top of the entire outfit. A full bird Colonel. He gave me a lecture about how I had better straighten up, and then he denied my leave.

"Yes, sir. I understand, sir. I feel I must inform you, sir, that I am going to exercise my right and write to the Inspector General."

He looked at me for the first time. He gave me his best "threatening stare." It was obvious that he worked on it a lot. "Well, all right, Airman, if you think you must. That letter will go into your record." But this was not really a big deal. He and the Inspector General would see each other at the Officer's Club one evening and straighten the whole thing out without ever having to talk to me again.

"Yes, sir. Thank you sir. I must also inform you, sir, that I am going to exercise my rights and write to my Senator."

"WHAT! YOU'RE GOING TO DO WHAT!"

That was a very big deal.

You see, if I wrote a letter to my Senator, and he made a five minute phone call, then some poor officer in Montana or somewhere else had to fill out months of paper work, and it could become a "Black Mark" on his record and maybe result in a Congressional Inquiry.

"WHAT, YOU'RE GOING TO DO WHAT!"

"Exercise my rights to write."

"Exercising your asshole. You don't know your rights from your asshole."

"Yes, sir, but," I started to talk as fast as I could in order to get in as much as possible before he cut me off. I continued: "I am going to write Senator Vincent, sir. Senator Vincent used to be just good old rancher Vincent, and my father sold him his very first family life insurance policy. Funny how those two old guys got along, and I became Senator Vincent's godson. And when I am not at my brother's wedding, he'll miss me, and when he finds out it is because my commander won't let me come, well . . . "

"SHUT UP, STOWELL!"

"Yes, sir."

"Is any of that bullshit true?"

"Yes, sir. Some of it, sir. Enough of it, sir!"

"You little smartass. Do you know what your problem is? You're a goddamn pointy-headed intellectual. You read too many goddamn books. What was that book I saw you reading yesterday? The one with the bright red cover."

"Oh, that one, sir. It was the *Communist Manifesto* by Karl Marx."

"WHAT, you were reading what? You have to have a top secret security clearance to get into this building, and the *Communist Manifesto* does NOT have a top secret security clearance."

"Yes, sir. I was just trying to learn how the enemy thinks. As General Clausewitz suggests."

"What?"

"General Clausewitz, the Polish General."

"Goddamn you, I know who Clausewitz is. I graduated from the Air Force Academy."

"Yes, sir. I know, sir."

"You son-of-a-bitch. You're a goddamn smartass. All the other officers tell me all the time, you are nothing but a goddamn smartass."

"Yes, sir. I know, sir. I try to be dumber than some of the officers, but sometimes I simply can't manage it."

"SHUT UP."

The veins in his neck were standing out. He shot out of his chair like he had been given an electric shock. He sat back down and slowly regained control of himself. He studied me. I was at attention so I couldn't look directly at him.

"Write your Senator, huh? You would." He paused. I imagined a small mean smile on his face.

"All right, Airman Stowell, I'll give you your leave. You don't have to write your Senator. Leave approved." And he signed my leave with such an enthusiastic flourish that he tore the paper.

"Happy now? I am. You want to know why I am happy?" His voice was barely audible, a raspy whisper, as if he were being squeezed. "I'll tell you why I'm happy. Because you are a fuck-up, Stowell, a natural born fuck-up, and you will fuck up again. Oh, maybe not on this leave, but sooner or later you will fuck up, and when you do, Stowell, I'll be waiting. I'll be waiting, and when that time comes, and it will come, I will be waiting, and you had better give your soul to God because your ass is going to belong to ME. Now get the fuck out of my office."

"Yes, sir." I was smiling as I left. And I got out of his office, and I had gone all the way to Texas, and then to Kansas City, and now I was going to the stockade thinking, there's going to be one very happy Colonel back in Great Falls, Montana.

We arrived at the stockade, which didn't look very big from the outside. I was turned over to an older, very large friendly-looking black sergeant. He typed out the form.

"OK, kid," he said. "It's Friday night."

I said, "What does that mean? Do I win some sort of a prize?"

He stopped typing and looked at me, not altogether unkindly, and said, "Shut up. Don't be a smartass kid. You're in jail now. Your ass gets smart, it gets beat."

"Sorry," I said. "Thanks."

"Uh huh. Anyway it is Friday night, so I can't check you into the bull pen, into the general population, until Monday morning. See, if anything was to happen to you then the shit would come down on my head, and there is no way that is going to happen, kid. On Monday morning, you can be officially checked in, and then if you get killed in the bull pen, it is OK because you are official. Do you know what I mean?"

"Ya, sarge, I do." And I did. He was practicing the number one rule of any enlisted man anywhere: CYA, cover your ass.

"Do you know what the bull pen is, kid?"

"Yes I do, I think you mean a sort of dormitory-type room, bunk beds, like a barracks?"

"Ya, I thought you might. Anyway, I am going to have to put you in a holding cell. This is a small jail. We don't have any real holding cells here, so I am going to have to put you in one of the solitary cells. We only have two, and there is someone in the other cell."

"Thanks," I said and meant it.

He looked at me and something seemed to soften in his face.

"Listen, kid, I'll give you a piece of advice. The guards down in the jail in the cell block really don't like that guy in the other solitary cell, so whatever you do, whatever happens—don't talk to him. Got it?"

"Yes, sir. Thanks a lot."

"Uh huh. I'll tell them that you are not down in that solitary cell for punishment, just for holding, so they can turn your light off at night."

He typed some more.

I thought: turn off my light? I said, "Gee thanks. I would never have thought of that."

"Uh huh, and I'll tell them not to wake you when they wake the other guy."

"When's that?"

"4:30 a.m."

"Ah, thanks a lot. I appreciate that."

"Sure. You don't look like a half bad kid."

He then escorted me down the hall through some locked doors, down stairs, and, as we were going along, he said, "One thing I should tell you about, kid. Down here in the cell block, the two jailers run the place. I can't help you one bit. If you piss them off, there won't be anybody who can help you. Got that?"

"I think so."

"Uh huh." He handed me over to the first jailer, a guy with a shaved head, sloping shoulders and large hips. In fact, his hips seemed to be larger than his shoulders, and his feet somehow seemed larger than his hips. He looked like one of those toys that bounce right back up, *booiiing* when you hit them. He was 6'5" tall and weighed about 270 pounds. His forehead sloped down, forming a sort of shelf that hooded his eyes. They were the color of greasy ball bearings. He had huge hands, the size of hams. His name was Raymond.

The other jailer was 5'11" tall. His uniform looked newly pressed and his hair was neatly trimmed. He had a tiny cheap shoe salesman mustache and beautiful robin's-egg-blue eyes. His name was Raymond.

Raymond and Raymond. They had never met before the Air Force brought them together and made them jailers.

They took me down to the solitary cell. A steel door with a tiny window covered in a fine wire mesh. Inside was a stainless steel toilet, stainless steel bunk, and one light bulb on the twelve foot high ceiling, covered with the same wire mesh.

I had already started calling them big Raymond and little Raymond in my mind. Big Raymond said to me, "We put the food in the slot in the door." His voice seemed to match his body perfectly. Prehistoric.

"Don't talk," he said.

I thought about reminding him I wasn't down here for punishment, but I didn't want to put any ideas into his head, and the look on his face scared the shit out of me. Little Raymond turned out the light and slammed the cell door shut.

How can I explain the sound of the slamming of a cell door? A sound that has such an incredible visceral impact. A sound that doesn't go through your brain as much as through your bowels. The sound of opening and closing cell doors, the beginning or the end of hope. I hadn't slept in two days, so when I lay down I went to sleep with no problem.

The next morning at 4:30, Big Raymond woke up the guy next door. If they caught him sitting on his bunk between 4:30 a.m. and 7:00 p.m., they gave him what Big Raymond later described to me as "specialty PT. Knuckle drill." I figured out what that meant by taking one look at Big Raymond's hands.

Breakfast Saturday was passed through the slot in the door. I did not talk. I was grateful for breakfast, but not because of the food. I was in solitary, so I got bread and water, but not real bread. A special loaf. It consisted of all the left-overs from the chow hall from the day before, ground-up and mixed together, shaped into a loaf and baked. That and a large cup of water. But I was grateful because now I had some idea what time it was. I did not own a watch. Never wanted one. Time had never been important to me before. Suddenly it was.

My sense of time began to become distorted. I measured my cell: two steps, turn, two steps, turn.

I walked. I meditated. I exercised.

I paced: two steps, turn, two steps, turn, until I was exhausted. After breakfast, I went back to pacing: two steps, turn, two steps, turn.

I wondered what the guy next door was doing? What was he in for? Why did the jailers dislike him so much? Two steps, turn, two steps, turn. I couldn't hear anything.

There was nothing to write on. Nothing to read. Nothing to see. Nothing to listen to. No radio or television. My sense of time got more and more out of whack.

Two steps, turn, two steps, turn. I was pacing faster now. I had never been alone before. Not like this.

Of course, I had been alone; anyone can be alone. You just

go into your room, shut the door, and you are alone, and if you want to be unalone, you just open the door, or walk out onto the street, or go to a bar, and there is the bartender and you are no longer alone.

Two steps, turn, two steps, turn. My heart beat faster. I was sweating. I can't open this door and go outside, so I am completely alone, and nothing I can do will change that. Nothing here but me. Nobody here but me. Two steps, turn, two steps, turn.

Saturday night, I dreamed of drowning. I woke up gasping for air, stumbled over to the door, and stuck my mouth to that little window covered with fine wire mesh and tried to suck in the air from the hallway. Finally I had enough air to be able to get my heart beat down enough so I could lie down again. I dozed off. I woke up drenched in sweat, gasping for air, my heart beating so fast it felt like it was about to push right out of my body. I staggered to the door and tried to get some more air.

Sunday morning and thank God for breakfast! Once again, I had some idea of the time. This is my last island of solid time. We get no lunch or dinner. My sense of time goes completely out of whack. Minutes pass and I think it has been hours. Hours go by and I think it has been minutes. I lose complete control of my sense of time.

Now it seemed that my mind was on full ahead flush. It was a perpetual motion thought machine. Never one second's rest. Not one split second of peace. I remember fragments of song, the same part of a verse over and over and over again. TV advertisements, jingles, conversations I never had, arguments that I lost and now I win, over and over again.

Two steps and turn, two steps and turn. Faster and faster, in tempo with my mind which is beginning to feel the way a car engine sounds when it is being badly over-strained. My thought began to flow out of my head into bubbles, like in cartoons. Thought bubbles. But the thought bubbles don't go anywhere. A thought would form and instantly be replaced by another, but the first did not go away. It was just pushed aside.

Two steps, turn, two steps, turn. The cell began to fill up with my thought bubbles. I couldn't breathe. I couldn't stop my mind. Oh, please keep moving. I felt as if I was being crushed by the weight of all those thoughts, and there were more coming every second. I was like an old clown trying to keep up many plates spinning on the end of thin sticks. I was running around inside of my head trying to keep all my plates spinning, but now the spinning plates had taken on a life of their own and I couldn't control them. Some kept spinning and spinning and others fell and broke, no matter how hard I tried to stop them.

I was bouncing off the walls of my cell and found myself speaking out-loud saying, "Come on, Jim, only 14 or 15 more hours to go," and then I laughed, "hahahaha" demonically.

I asked myself: How in the hell do you know that? You don't know what time it is. You'll never live through another night like last night. Hold on, Jim, hold on! Don't talk about not being able to make it. Hold on, Jim. Remember those old movies you saw with Jimmy Cagney and Edward G. Robinson? Remember how they used to say to the guys, *Listen you mugs, when youse in solitary, whatever happens don't start screaming, see. Once you start screaming, you can't ever stop. Remember that youse mugs.* And a wild high-pitched laugh exploded out of my body. "And you know what," I yelled. "It's true, it's true, goddamn it. If I start screaming, I'll never stop!" Tears were streaming down my face, but they seemed far away.

I'm still trying to pace, but my thought bubbles have taken over the cell, and I am struggling against them. Don't scream, don't scream, Jim. If you do, Big Raymond will come down here and beat the shit out of you. Oh, no, I don't want that. Oh please, God, don't let that happen. He would kill me with those hands. No, don't scream, Jim. Don't break, hold on.

Welling up inside of me is a white-hot panic. This panic, this fear, fills my brain and my body until it is all I can see, hear, think or be. I can hear, as if from a great distance, a small scream start to come out of my mouth, and my hands fly up like spirits with minds of their own, driven by a primal drive to survive, and cover my mouth. The panic builds, feeds on itself, the scream builds in sound, and from somewhere inside of me, a voice says, "Don't scream, Jim. Sing!" and the sound pushed my hands out of the way and exploded out of my mouth.

Be bop a lula, she's my baby.
Be bop a lula, I don't mean maybe.
Be bop a lula, she's my baby now.
My baby now, my baby now, my baby now.

Oh, yes, don't scream, sing. Singing is all right. Singing is American.

Oklahoma, and the wind comes racing across the plains.
Oklahoma where the blam floups houpy 'cross the trains.

Oh, ya, singing. Singing is ok.

Whole lotta shakin going on.
Whop bop a lu bop.
A lop bam boom.

What, what, what. Oh, dear God. My head is empty. My body continues to reel and career around the cell and my tempo increases as my mind spins out of control. My mind had gone completely blank. All day, no, for the last goddamn two days, my mind had been driving me crazy, and now it had gone completely blank. A howling blackness, a void that I fall down.

This is worse, oh worse. This is worse. I'm crawling across the cell floor. Rolling and crawling and then my hand over my mouth. *Aaaaaaaahhhhhhhhggggggghhh.* Inside, there is a siren roaring. Red lights flashing and the smell of burning rubber. Sing anything, anything. Camp songs. Oh, yes, camp songs. But what? What? *Aaaaaaahhhhhhhhgggggglllll.* Little bunny fufu, hopping through the forest, picking up the field mice.

Bop them on the head.
Down comes the good fairy.
Little bunny fofo, I don't want to see you.
Picking up the field mice.
And bopping them on the head.
And the good fairy flew back into the sky.
The next day.
Little bunny fofo, picking up the field mice, bops them on the head.
Bop, bop, bop.
Bop, bop, bop.
Whop, bop a lu bop.
Got a gal named Daisy,
Sure do drive me crazy.
She knows how to love me.
Yes, indeed.

And the guy in the next cell, who I haven't heard a word from for two days, starts to sing right along with me.

Whop bop a lu bop, a lop bam boom.
Whop bop a lu bop.
A lop bam boom.
Got a gal named Daisy,
Sure do drive me crazy.

He is inspired and takes off on Country and Western tunes, and then into something that sounds like reruns of *I Love Lucy* shows.

I'm inflamed. I have a partner. I began to sing what we call in my family "classic Italiano operatic shower singing."

Mogo pogo mancha I panchi ma.
Gomo hojo wanchi canche wa
Ha ha ha ha ha.

The guy in the next cell joined me again. This particular kind of singing was indigenous to my family, but he joined me as if he had grown up next door to me and we had known each other all our lives.

Pogo molo cancho rancho da
Rollo pollo koko dancho za
Ha ha ha ha ha ha.

Boom! The door to the end of the cell block slammed open. I could hear Raymond and Raymond come through the door fast. I stopped singing instantly. Not the guy in the cell next to me. He got wilder.

Yaaaaaahhhhhhhhggggggggaaaahhhh sa sa
Ahhhhhhhyyyyywawawayeeahh!
Yeecchh! Aghagh.
Dori mi la ti ma fa sooooooo

I could hear his cell door open but that didn't stop him.

Whhhheeeerrrrrrggggrrrraaaaggggghhheeeeooo
Ooooohhhhgggg

Pow! I could hear Big Raymond hit the guy. Umph. I could hear the sound of Big Raymond's fist hitting the guy's body and the explosion of breath out of the body and the involuntary grunt of pain. The sound of his being hit in the face was distinctly different from the sound of his being hit in the body. The sounds of the beating came through the cell wall very clearly.

I heard his cell door close. I backed away from my cell door. I heard them walk to my cell. My back was against the wall. I heard the key in the cell door.

I was thinking: "What in the hell am I going to do? Dear God, what am I going to do? Am I going to fight back? Am I going to fight Raymond? He'll kill me if I do. Fighting back will just piss him off," and the door swung open. "Or am I going to take it? Roll over like an old dog and just take it? What in the hell am I going to do?

Big Raymond filled the door and stepped into the cell. His knuckles were skinned and bloody. I could just barely see little Raymond's face, but I could tell that I wasn't going to get any help from him. Our eyes met. He shrugged his shoulders. "I can't stop him when he gets going," Little Raymond told me later.

Big Raymond pointed at me. His other hand was in a fist held up to show me. "You," he said. "You started this shit." He pointed again. "Cut that shit out, got it?"

"Yeah." I was hoarse with fear.

He snorted, "Yeah," mimicking me. He looked at Little Raymond. "Yeah," he snorted again. He turned to go, then whirled around and our eyes met. He game me a look of bottomless stark hatred. We were frozen for a second. He whirled around again and slammed the cell door shut behind him. I could hear them walking down the hallway, their shoes echoing in the cell block. Then I heard the cell block door open and close, and they were gone. I stood and trembled. I felt like a safe had just dropped twenty storeys and missed hitting me on the head by one inch. I heard a groan from the next cell.

I crawled over to the wall and tapped. "Can you hear me?" I whispered. "I'll get you a doctor, man. Do you need a doctor? Can you hear me? Can you hear me, man?"

Another groan and then, "Yeah I can hear you. Can you hear me?"

"Yeah, yeah, I can hear you. Do you need a doctor, man? We'll make them get you a doctor." I could tell from his voice that he was in a lot of pain. "Yeah, I can hear you."

"Good, good," he said. "Listen, fuck you."

"What? What?" I said.

"Fuck you, man. Fuck you, aaahhh," he groaned, and I could hear his body slump over.

"Fuck me, fuck me, what, what?" I backed across the cell. I squatted in the corner and rocked back and forth until the adrenalin wore off and I fell asleep on the floor.

When I woke up, it was Monday morning, and I was never so glad to see a bunch of cons and clerks in my whole life.

The guys in the bull pen were from the base and in for petty crimes, like me. On Monday morning, after breakfast, they marched off to their regular jobs and then marched back in the evening. They spent their evenings and weekends in jail. So during the day I was left alone with Raymond and Raymond. Big Raymond ignored me. I was glad.

I spent most of my time on different "details." For instance, "head detail." Cleaning the bathrooms. All of my "details" entailed cleaning the stockade in one way or another. I pushed a broom, a mop, and a toilet brush. There was a tremendous amount of paper work about me going back and forth between the two air bases, most of which I never saw, and had nothing to do with me. But occasionally I would have to cross the base and sign some paper and then march back to my jail. My escort on these little escapades was always Little Raymond. We talked. He seemed like a normal person from someplace in the Midwest.

Thursday I was on trash detail. That meant I was pushing a large metal platform with five or six metal trash cans on it. I was going to dump all the trash in the dumpsters, which were fifty feet outside the stockade. So Little Raymond was with me at the back gate behind the other buildings, all alone, and no one likely to come by. Completely out of sight. He took out the keys to the lock on the back gate and started to unlock it.

He was telling me about the telephone conversation he had overhead this morning between his commander and my commander. "Oh man," he said, "it looks bad for you, Jim. They were laughing like hell. Man, Jim, that guy up there is really laying for you."

"Ya, I told you he would be," I said. But I wasn't too worried because the stockade back in Great Falls was a very low key sort of place. I would probably know most of the people there.

He had the gate unlocked.

"No shit. I'm serious, man. Jim, this is serious. I heard them say that you are going to be sent to Leavenworth."

"Leavenworth! Leavenworth is a federal penitentiary, a place for murders and rapists."

"Yeah," he said. And he opened the gate so I could see outside. "But you've already been busted twice. You are now a three time loser. You told me that yourself."

"Yes," I said.

"So, you're going to Leavenworth."

"That's impossible, Raymond. Leavenworth is for murders and rapists."

"That's right, Jim. But you pissed off a full bird colonel. You pissed off one of the good old boys. That means you pissed them all off. You know how it works."

The gate was wide open.

"Your commander will call up one of his pals that he was stationed with in some godforsaken hole ten thousand years ago, and that old buddy will throw your ass in Leavenworth federal penitentiary for eighteen months for conduct unbecoming and AWOL."

"Jesus Christ, Raymond, I was only two days AWOL. Two days! And I turned myself in."

"Bull shit. That doesn't matter, and you know it. If your commander wants you to go someplace bad enough, then that is where you are going to end up. You know how the system works. You're going to Leavenworth for eighteen months and end up staying for the rest of your life. One of those murders or rapists will try to murder or rape you, and you will either have to become somebody's candy baby, kill somebody, or be carried out feet first."

He look around. "Listen kid," he said. He took hold of my arm and stepped into the opening of the gate but not quite outside it. "You're a nice kid. Don't let them screw up your entire life because of one little mistake. I know what I am talking about. You will go to that place for eighteen months and stay for life. Man, Jim, what do you think solitary is like in there?"

The idea froze my brain with fear.

"See those dumpsters?" he pointed at them.

"Yeah."

"See that line of trees beyond them?"

"Yeah."

"Through those trees is the fence to the air base. A piece of cake. You will be over it in a couple of minutes."

"Yeah."

"Sure," he said. "Then you go through another set of trees and there is a country road that takes you right into Kansas City. From there you can get to Mexico. Be smart, Jim. Don't let them destroy your entire life because they are a bunch of assholes. Make a run for it."

I looked at the trees. I thought about solitary in Leavenworth prison.

I felt his grip tighten on my arm. His voice went up in pitch. "Come on, Jim. We haven't got all day. Don't worry about me. I'm on your side. I'll tell you what I'll do. I'll give you all the way to the dumpsters."

"What? You'll do what, Raymond?"

"I'll give you all the way to the dumpsters."

I noticed that the flap was open on his pistol. He was wearing one of those old Army .45 automatics, huge slugs. If it hits you in the foot, it tears your foot off, and you die of the shock. He noticed me looking at his pistol and started to laugh.

"Hell, Jim, don't worry about this thing." He patted the gun. "You couldn't hit an elephant with this thing at that distance."

"Wait a minute, Raymond. I want to get this straight. I mean, I would hate to have a misunderstanding at a time like this. You will give me all the way to those dumpsters before you pull out your pistol and shoot at me. Is that the deal?"

"Yeah. I won't clear leather until you get past there." He pointed at the dumpsters. Then he laughed again and there was something cracked about it. "Buffalo Bill himself couldn't hit you with this thing," he patted his pistol again, "at that distance. Come on Jim, we haven't got all day." He was sort of pulling on my arm trying to edge me out the gate. "Make a run for it," he said. I looked closely at him out of the corner of my eye, and I could see that mustache twitching and those robin's-egg-blue eyes spinning backwards.

A voice was screaming inside my head, "Don't go outside this gate. Do not go outside this gate. Do not. Do not."

I could see it very clearly. I would step outside the gate, get a few steps away, I would hear something and turn. There would be Little Raymond with his pistol out, pointed at my head. The sound I would hear was the cocking of the pistol. There would now be a shell in the chamber. I would see his eyes looking down the barrel of the gun, and then he would say to me, "You should have known better than to trust someone like me, Jim. Bye-bye." Boom, and off flies the top of my head, and I am very dead. I am shot trying to escape. Little Raymond was just doing his duty. He wouldn't get into trouble. Hell, he might get promoted! Oh, no, do not go outside the stockade.

He was tightening his grip on my arm, still trying to edge me out the gate. "Come on, Jim," he said. "What are you waiting for? Someone might come. Go!"

What could I say to him? That I can't go out dressed like this, or that I left the keys to my car back in my cell? What, what can I say to him? If I say the wrong thing he could shoot me right here.

"You think I'm crazy, don't you."

"Oh no, Raymond, not that, never. I just can't go right now."

"You can't? What do you mean you can't?"

The inside of my head is an explosion of a mirror factory. My mouth opens and the words fly out. "I can't, Raymond, because I got to take a shit."

"You're what, you're chicken shit? I'm going to . . . "

"Oh, no, that's not it. You don't understand. It's the prison food. The food has so much grease. All that grease. I have had the runs all day. The last two days. I've really got to take a shit. It's just nature. Nature is calling, Raymond?" Pause. "It's the food, Raymond." I felt I was teetering on the brink. He looked at me.

"Yeah," he said. "The food here is hell. Everybody gets the shits here sooner or later, except me." Then he laughed again. "Come on, we wouldn't want you to shit your pants."

We turned and walked inside. I hadn't noticed how far we had gotten outside of the jail gate. He locked the gate. As we were walking away, he stopped suddenly and grabbed me again.

"Listen man, I'm not crazy, I'm not crazy."

"Oh no, Raymond, it's just the chow. I mean it was a great idea, but nature is calling, Raymond."

"Oh yeah, come on." And as we were walking through the stockade he told me about how Big Raymond had told him just the day before, "I thought I was going to shit my brains out." He did a perfect imitation of Big Raymond's voice. Little Raymond thought the whole thing was funny because, "it never happens to me. I grew up on food just like this stuff."

The trash was not taken out that day.

The next morning a clerk came to my cell and told me I was being sent back to my home base "under my own recognisance." He gave me a train ticket and food voucher and said, "You will be driven into town to the train station. One of the regular patrol officers will drive you in."

I walked down into the prison garage a very happy man. When I got in the front door of the police car, I saw that the driver was Little Raymond. We looked at each other.

"I thought one of the regular patrol officers was going to drive me into town."

"I volunteered," he said, his blue eyes looking like a scout master's. This is the way he would look when he was explaining to his commanding officer how I had tried to escape, make a break for it. He would even have a little bruise on his forehead from where I had tried to overpower him so he had to blast me right in the car.

And then Big Raymond got into the car. I was never so glad to see that monster in my life. Oh yeah, I think. He won't kill me in front of another cop. Oh yeah, he might try to trick me if we were by ourselves, but not in front of another cop, not in front of a witness. We drove off the base through the country towards Kansas City. Wait a minute, I thought. What do I mean, another cop. The three of us sitting in the front seat of the car with me in the middle. Raymond and Raymond, I think, are the same cop, and every time we came to a little road, I would pray, oh Lord, don't let us turn down this road.

Nothing happened. We didn't turn down any of those side roads. I was never so glad to see a train station in my whole life. We went inside to wait for the train. I sat in the in the middle. I wondered if they ever double-dated, and if they sat like this on their dates. It was an old fashioned train station with cathedral-high ceilings, marble floors, a perfect echo chamber. We sat and listened for my train to be announced.

Train leaving on track Ungh for
Rosnogcrarmairnarghtyompzempzar, last call please.

We sat. Finally Big Raymond said to me, "I guess you want to know about the other guy in solitary, huh?"

I knew this was not just a story but a message I was to take away with me.

"Yes," I said. "Tell me about him. What's his name?" Big Raymond ignored that.

"Routine patrol," he said. "Checked his papers. AWOL from the Navy, Great Lakes."

You see, in all the large towns where there were large military bases nearby, the military police made regular checks of all the bus stations and airports, and they asked to see your leave papers. And it was really easy, after awhile, to spot guys who were in the military.

Big Raymond went on. "He was busted. They brought him to us. We liked him. We were nice to him. He ran. That makes us look bad. A black mark on our records. They caught him again two weeks later, right here in this train station. The same place as before. He was waiting for a train. Some guys never learn, huh? They brought him back to Raymond and me."

And at this point, the volume of his voice dropped a little, and we were all leaning in, heads almost touching. "We gave him some knuckle drill, you know what I mean?"

I saw very clearly Raymond's bloody knuckles as he stepped into my cell after beating the guy next door.

"Yes," I said. "I know what you mean."

"I'll bet. You're kind of smart. That guy, they caught him twice in the same spot. You would never make that mistake, would you?"

"No, Raymond. You'll never catch me in the same place twice."

"Good for you. You want to know what is going to happen to that guy next?"

"Well, all right, what?"

Big Raymond looked at me. "He's going to be put on 'trash detail,' and I bet he ain't as smart as you." Then he made a sound that must have been laughing. I turned to look at Little Raymond. His robin's-egg-blue eyes were shining; he was smiling like a used car salesman.

They put me on the train. Then, like a gymnastic team, they jumped off the moving train and landed nimbly on the platform. They were surprisingly graceful. The train slowly pulled out, and we looked at each other. Something primeval overtook all of us.

Some sort of primeval instinct, and all our arms flew up and we waved good bye to each other. Our arms flapped, bye-bye.

And then I flashed on a conversation I had with Little Raymond as we were walking across the base together. I said, "Raymond, I don't think I'm cut out for the Air Force or any other branch of the service."

"I think you're right," he said, "but I am. I'm a lifer. I'm going to be right here doing this job in this way until I retire. The next twelve years."

Bye-bye Kansas City.

Bye-bye, Raymond and Raymond.

Cascading

I'm getting out of the back of a new government issue pickup truck. I jump out of the back of the truck onto a dirt road. A mountain road high in the eastern Sierras of California. I pull my backpack out, the truck pulls away, and I wave good-bye to the Forest Service driver who I've never seen before. He waved good-bye to me, and we never see each other again. I put my backpack on, and I'm ready to go camping, but I swear someone has been sneaking large rocks into my pack when I wasn't looking. Or maybe even an anvil.

The year is 1979. I am thirty-one years old. I am running away from the city. Running away from a failed romance. Entirely my fault and I knew it. Away from the frustrations of my work. I had recently come to grips with the fact that my fantasies about working in the theater were more deeply rooted than I thought.

I had come to these mountains to recharge my batteries. And to heal. Over the last six years, these mountains had become my place of healing.

My brother Lorenzo showed me a canyon the year before, telling me, "Right off the road, and no one ever goes in there. It's too steep. Jim, there are places in that canyon that haven't seen a human face in over fifty years. In those places, you will be able to hear things. See things. Hear the mountain sing. And, maybe, the spirits of the mountains will show themselves to you. The mountain will always teach you the lesson you need to know." He laughed. "And it might help you kick those big city blues."

Then he grinned at me, that same grin I had been looking at since I was a little boy. Now he had a full black beard and long black hair over the collar of a T-shirt that had nothing written on it. He was smiling the same smile that had always been protecting and challenging me.

"Just follow the water. Keep going up."

I start to hike up a trail that runs beside the river. I hike up the canyon, following the river for two days. At the start of the third day, I begin to follow a major side-stream up another canyon. I camp at the fork of that stream and another stream and go to sleep listening to the meeting of the two streams. I have been alone all this time. Haven't seen a single person, and I am absolutely thriving on it.

I leave behind my base camp, pack light and begin to follow the smaller stream up the side of the mountain. My plan is to follow that stream to its very source, wherever that might be. To keep going up the stream until it is a snowbank dripping one drop at a time, forming a tiny trickle on its way to the Pacific Ocean, or maybe a spring bubbling up out of the earth. I'm going to follow that water to its source and drink from it.

I climb all day until I am at about 11,000 feet, above the tree line. I scramble over a ridge, and there is a slab of granite that must be forty or fifty yards wide, one hundred fifty yards long, on a steep slope. Because the slope is solid granite, the water does not form one narrow stream but spreads across the face of the rock, forming a cascade. The water was like silver cloud curtains, dancing, covering the window of stone.

I lay beside the cascade and listened. I took off all my clothes and draped my tired old bones on that granite warm from the sun, and I rolled over and lapped the water like a dog with my butt sticking up to the sky.

I looked across the sheet of water and saw a pair of shoes. A pair of spats with water breaking over them. I looked further up and saw pants, striped. A man was standing in the middle of the cascade staring at me. He was wearing a cutaway coat, ascot, striped vest, and a top hat, a very tall stovepipe top hat. The suit was striped red, white and blue. He had a little goatee. Every time he moved, the stripes moved, changed, bled into one another and apart again. The suit shimmered and flashed in the sunlight like a bird's belly. The top hat was full of arrows. I don't mean Indian arrows but directional arrows. Road sign arrows, moving and pointing in many directions at the same time. Also, arrows pointing out from under his coat, out of his vest, out of his pants legs, from under his collar. Popping out all over him. Pointing every which way. Then all of those arrows were pointing at me. He laughed a high-pitched cackle. A wicked witch's laugh. I had seen all the movies when I was a kid, and I recognized that kind of laugh when I heard it. I was afraid. I was down on my hands and knees with my butt sticking into the air like a turned-over teacup. I never felt so insignificant, so completely ridiculous.

At that second, a Stellar's blue jay flew between us. The Stellar jays are the pranksters of the forest. The jokers. The harlequinos of the backwoods. They practically take the food off the end of your fork. They have a raucous laugh-like caw, a great bar-room laugh. When I saw that blue jay and heard his caw, I just had to laugh. I stuck my face down into the ice cold cascade water, put my nose right on the granite. All I could hear was the roar of the water, the song of the mountain. I felt the water run down my face and chest. I sat up and felt the breeze on my chest, the sunlight on my face, and I felt good. I just had to laugh. I opened my eyes and the man in the suit was gone.

I leaned down to drink again, lapping it up. I shot up to sit. My ears were open, my nose open. I don't mean to say that I had an increased sense of smell in the sense that I could smell a pine tree from a mile away. Oh no. I could smell tomorrow's weather. Each and every smell carried with it a physical imperative that ran throughout my entire body like an electric current. Messages like, do I eat it or does it eat me?

And then I was back on the side of the mountain at the cascade, looking across the water at eye level. At that moment I felt an incredible yearning. I didn't even know for what, but the feeling was so overwhelming that I felt it was going to pull my heart right out of my body. As I looked across that cascade, I could see that every rock, every tree, the water, everything that I could see was in exactly the right place, in the perfect place for it to be at that moment in nature.

Everything was in exactly the right place for it to be at that time, including me.

And then it passed, that feeling. It simply left me. Just like that. Nothing spectacular, nothing more spectacular than opening your hand.

Now I was just a regular guy on the side of the mountain getting a drink of water.

The Big Blue Thing

1

The year is 1986, and I was driving a 1968 Chrysler Imperial LeBaron—a boat of a car with electric everything. There are small drawbacks, however. The heat never goes off, and crossing the Mojave desert, this becomes somewhat distracting. Two-tone blue, it's known as The Big Blue Thing.

I passed through Los Angeles, affectionately known as The Toilet, and I am driving out of Bakersfield, where I get the feeling that everyone in town is trying to get out of town as fast as possible, and I am one of them. I am headed for Highway 395 north towards the Owens Valley in eastern California. There are some wide open spaces on this route and on the rest of my trip through New Mexico and Arizona and Texas.

Once again I listen very closely to the sounds the car is making. All the sounds. I bought The Big Blue Thing from a friend of mine in Minneapolis for $150, three-and-a-half months ago, and I said to him that I was going to try to drive it to California and back.

He said, "I don't know, Jim." He is an honest man and made me no promises. I drove it there, drove it around the mountains for three months, and was on my way back to Rosemount, Minnesota, my home.

I was heading across some wide open spaces. By now, I was familiar with all the sounds of the car, but I knew that my luck could change at any second. I hear the old familiar *nnnnnddddddddnnnnnddddd*. And I hear the *didididididididdidid*. The car has been making these sounds since I started, and we are still rolling, so I figure they must be okay. While I am listening for new ones or ones just as bad, the old sound changes. The old *nnnnnddddddddnnnnnndddddd* becomes *eeeeeeeeeeeeeeeeeeeee!* No one has to send you to music school for you to know that when the sound goes up in pitch, you have a serious problem.

I am feeling the ride of The Big Blue Thing, as if the entire car has becomes an extension of my body. I can feel the road up through the steering wheel.

At the same time I am running through a mental check list: "Tires, bad, but I've got a pretty good spare; oil, transmission fluid; fan belt. I wonder why the car dies every time I let the engine idle?"

What happens way out here in the middle of nowhere if the *nnnnnnndddddddddnnnnndddd* starts to go *eeeeeeeeeeeeeeee! Brrannnggg!* And then the car just stops. What can I do to fix it? Could I look under the hood and figure out what is wrong? No. I could not. What can I do? I can change a tire. Yep. That's about it.

I feel pretty stupid, but I bet that if I could stop these passing cars and ask the people inside if they could fix their cars, the answer, if honest, would be no. How many hours have we spent looking under the hood of a car and putting that look on, the one that means you actually know what the hell is going on under there? People stand around and fake it. Someone finally says: "sounds like the tappets." Uh, huh.

We love our cars. We screw in them. Thousands of happy homes are started in the backseats of cars. We name them. They become like members of our family. We are born in them. We live in them. We are even buried in them. But we can't fix them. All we can do is shine them.

This failure is part of a giant conspiracy, the one between the auto makers and the school system. Why in the hell doesn't the school system teach us how to fix our cars? Why waste a lot of time on some of the crap they teach instead of showing us how to take care of the thing we spend so much of our time in and with. They should start in the first grade.

Our cars have become so complex that only a select few people can look under the hood of the car and have a prayer of an idea of what is making that *rrrrrrrggggggggghhhhhhhpppppp*. They are called auto mechanics, the high priests of our time. When you take your car to the Temple, it doesn't matter who you are or how rich you are. The high priests have total power. As far as our cars are concerned, we are living in the Middle Ages.

2

I spent the last night in a little Texas town miles off the inter-state. I pulled into a little motel with at least half the letters in the neon sign out.

___AG___US __OT__L, it said, over and over again. The office is the living room of a cranky old man. As I registered I asked to see the room. He looked at me, smoke rising from his Chesterfield. He probably thought he looked like Bogart in some movie, fighting alone against all odds. He really looked more like a piece of beef jerky with eyes, and I loved his Texasness.

"See the room," he said. "What you want to see the goddamn room for? If you don't like the goddamn room, then I'll give you your goddamn money back."

"No, no, no," I said. "I know where I am now."

"You from Texas?"

"Yes, I am."

"Been gone long?"

"Yes."

He just shook his head and handed me the key.

"I suppose you want me to guide you to your room now."

I got up early in the morning and drove to a combination gas station and grain elevator. The old man who filled The Big Blue Thing with gas thought I looked too much like California, and my Minnesota license plate made me some kind of goddamn Yankee. I watched the sun rise through the dirty window panes of a north Texas gas station.

I pushed hard all day. No breakfast stop. No food stops at all. No rest stops. I pushed hard for Oklahoma City where I can turn north. I can smell home for the first time. I stop for gas, relieve myself, buy some juice and chocolate, and I am off. Sugar and coffee are what I need to cruise all day and into the night at 70 miles an hour.

Oklahoma City. It is huge in its width. It must be bigger than Lichtenstein. Finally, I'm headed north. This really changes the map dance. As I cross the country, I keep folding the map and now I am on the last fold.

Around 10 a.m., I stop in a small town in Missouri. I can hear the wings of a bird flying past the filling station. No other cars.

The filling station attendant is half asleep inside. I can hear the clicking of the gas pump and I yawn.

The roar of a semi-trailer truck—the roar of a sixteen wheeler going by in the opposite direction—snaps me awake. I must not sleep. I am in Missouri. If I drive all night, I can get home by tomorrow morning. I will not fall asleep behind the wheel as I did when I was nineteen.

I was hitchhiking across Nevada. A guy picked me up and said "I'll give you a ride, but you've got to drive so I can sleep. Can you do that?"

I said, sure. I drove for a couple of hours and, slowly, I began to doze off. I was supposed to keep driving, so I didn't stop or pull over. I fell asleep behind the wheel.

I woke up to hear a semi-truck roaring past at 90 miles an hour. When I woke, I was just past the point of collision. Split seconds before the sound of the truck woke me up, I was asleep at the wheel. It was sheer luck that I missed going into a head-on with that semi-truck, which would have killed both of us in that car, beyond any shadow of a doubt. That truck was so close I could have reached out the driver's window of that 1962 Buick and touched it with my elbow.

You've got to be lucky. If you travel around in these vehicles, then you've got to be lucky sometimes, but experience helps. I've never dozed off like that again.

During the night of the third day in The Big Blue Thing, I was wide awake.

3

I stopped in Des Moines, Iowa, almost home. Des Moines was my first real stop since I left that little town in Oklahoma yesterday morning. I stopped in an all-night fast food franchise place and I bought a piece of apple pie. I have eaten apple pie in almost every state of this union. For twenty years of hitchhiking and traveling across America and everywhere I go, I have eaten apple pie, testing apple pie across the country. I am a man who is willing to risk his life for apple pie.

My grandmother on my father's side of the family made the

world's greatest apple pies. The apples came from the tree in her yard. She sprinkled cinnamon and sugar on the top. When she made one of those pies, there was no promise I could keep, and everybody knew it. If I got hold of one of those pies, I would eat the whole thing like a hound dog gone crazy. I could be blocks away; I would smell one of those pies baking and take off.

My grandmother owned a large old-fashioned hutch full of generations of family glass and china. My grandmother would get out a small step-ladder, climb up to the top, put those pies on top of the hutch to cool, and she would lock the ladder away.

One day she baked three apple pies, put them on top of the hutch, locked the ladder away, and then poured herself a big glass of iced tea and joined my mother on the front porch swing.

The smell had drawn me to the kitchen. There were the pies. No one else was in the room. But first—I had to find out were the pie police were. I snuck out and saw my mother and grandmother on the front porch, the chief of pie police and the sheriff sitting together. All the important pie police in one spot. What a chance for me! Silently, I snuck back to the kitchen.

How to get to the top of that hutch? I had been climbing a lot of trees. I thought, why not?

The first step was easy. I pulled the chair over, stood on it, then climbed up onto the first landing. The door handles with those little round knobs. I put one toe on one of the door handles, grabbed the side of the hutch with my left hand and pulled up with my one hand, reached up and grabbed the ornate carving at the top with my right hand. I paused.

I was now balanced on my one toe, holding my hand on one side of the hutch, and with my other hand on the top. I could feel my balance. I planned. I pulled up and pushed up with my foot at the same time. I was going to reach up over the top and grab one of those pies with the hand I had been using to hold onto the side of the hutch. As I pulled and stood up, that movement changed the equilibrium. The hutch teetered forward and then back and then forward again. I wanted to scream for help, but in those seconds that the family glass and china rocked back and forth between safety and destruction, I still had hope of saving it. In my family, when you're not where you're supposed to be, there is no use calling out for help.

The hutch fell forward, full length on top of me. That was a lot of glass. I was cut in thousands of places, and that was the only thing that saved my life. When my mom and grandmother heard the crash, they came running. When they saw the hutch and the broken family glass my mother said to me years later, "we decided, instantly, to kill you on the spot. But you was bleeding too much."

I am a man who is willing to risk his life for apple pie.

I had a piece of apple pie in that place in Des Moines, Iowa, and it was glob. Over the last seven or eight years, the apple pie in America has turned to glob. You should be able to pull into any restaurant in this country and get a great piece of apple pie. Sure, you'd find a piece if you drove around and looked for hours, but you shouldn't have to do that. Good apple pie should be everywhere.

But the stuff that tastes like glob: use it for making buildings, but don't eat it. I ate it. And I drank the coffee. It was awful. What is happening to coffee in this country?

I drove out of Des Moines wondering about the state of coffee and apple pie in America today.

I drove the rest of the night and finally off Interstate 35 onto County Road 42 east. Then Highway 3 north. The sun was just beginning to rise. I cruise through Rosemount, Minnesota, the town still asleep except for the all-night filling station.

Half a mile outside of town, I take a left up a lane past a stand of pine trees. There is the barn with the old weather vane; the wind is from the south. I come blowing in with the breeze. I stop, turn off The Big Blue Thing. I asked it to get me to California and back, and it did. Good job, car. Damn good job, Big Blue Thing.

I get out of the car, open the back porch door, my kitchen door, and there, waiting for me is my cat Jesus, my dog Bear, and running down the stairs, around the corner into the kitchen, calling out my name with surprise and delight, her robe flying, eyes shining, the woman I love, my wife.

My cat is purring.

My dog is barking.

She is embracing me.

I am where every traveler longs to be.

I am home.

My Father's Hands
and the Owl's Eye

I'm walking in a thick woods near my home in Rosemount, Minnesota, just south of St. Paul. A late November day and the trees are bare of leaves. The clouds are very close to the earth. The sun's behind the clouds, so the sky is cast in grey shapes with stripes of grey. The trees with no leaves on them mark black, grey and white lines against the sky. I am walking through the woods on a trail that I have made over the years, walking with my dog Bear, my dog Bear. A black Lab.

She's fat now in her old age, and I call her the Secret Fat Potato. I watch her walk from behind, and she goes *dink-t-dink bomp, dink-t-dink bomp* because she is missing two toes on her left back paw. She chewed those two toes off to get herself out of a trap one January morning, years ago. Oh, there's a story, but there are many exciting stories about the Secret Fat Potato. I watch her walk, and I think, *Oh honey, you look fat on the outside, but you are mighty tough on the inside. I have never chewed off two of my toes, and I don't personally know of anybody who has done anything half as tough as that.*

Dink-t-dink bomp, dink-t-dink bomp, dink-t-dink bomp. Appearances are deceiving.

I was working on a play at the time, this play. So I was barely paying attention, just following Bear's lead. As I walked through the woods, I could see in front of me my notebooks on my desk. A yellow legal pad with handwritten notes. Notes about a trip down to Vero Beach, Florida, to see my parents when my father was still alive. Notes on the trip and especially the time the three of us spent together. And then I got out some letters from my father, written to me after the trip. I was reading the letters, and my eyes drifted over to my notes. I looked back at my notes and back at my father's handwriting. The js, the rs, the ts. Wait a minute.

I ran back to my desk and pulled out some of my old notebooks side-by-side-by-side. I looked at them, and the notes that were ten years old were clearly less like my father's handwriting than my more recent notes. I got right up from my desk, right into my boots, right out into the country, walking along behind Bear.

She stopped suddenly and looked up. My eyes followed hers, and as soon as I looked at it, a large owl flew out of the top of an elm tree. Flying right along with the large owl were two small black-colored birds calling out.

Eeekkkk! Eeekkk! Eeekkk! Eeekkk! A cutting, grating ragged-edged call. Calling as they flew through the woods.

An owl with a wingspread as wide as my arms. The owl glided into the top of a tall tree just a short distance away. The two small birds in trees flanked the owl. They continued to call intermittently. *Eeekkk! Eeekkk! Eeekkk!*

I crept over to get a better look at the owl sitting with its back to me. I could see the horns, grey and white against the grey, black and white sky and the dark lines of the tree. The owl was magnificent. I had a history with owls.

Eeekkk! Eeekkk! Eeekkk!

I looked at the black-colored birds. What were they doing in this beautiful picture?

Eeekkk! Eeekkk! Eeekkk! Eeekkk! Eeekkk! I realized that to me, the owl looked one way, but to them it looked entirely different. To them that owl was a predator. A carnivore. An owl ate mice and little birds, too. To those black birds, that owl was death. Death on the wing. Death fast and hard with claw and beak.

Eeekkk! Eeekkk! Eeekkk! Eeekkk! They called; *here's death, death's over here.* And when they flew through the woods, they flew on either side of the owl calling out, sounding the alarm. *Here's death, here it comes. Eeekkk! Eeekkk! Eeekkk!*

Why didn't the owl just chase them away? I wondered. But those big wings, it takes a while and some distance for the owl to pick up speed. I could see that staying in close to the owl is actually safer for the little birds. They had to stay very close but not too close, or, snatch, they're gone. What an exquisite and delicately balanced dance those little birds did with death.

Eeekkk! Eeekkk! Eeekkk!

At that moment, the owl swiveled its head. The owl's eye that could see a mouse moving a mile away, at night, looked directly at me. In the searchlight of its gaze, I had a vision of father's hands.

I could see my father's hands working. They were covered with grease. They were working with tools and they were working with machines; they were working with great competence and confidence. This was an extrordinary sight. I had never seen anything like this in my life with my father.

My father spent his entire life as a salesman. In the Rio Grande Valley, he was an insurance salesman. He was a terrific salesman, and he could teach other people to be good salesmen. He never fixed or puttered. When not selling, he was relaxing. He was a man who made his living by talking.

But the insurance company he worked for folded, and he and my mother had to pull up their roots and move to Florida, and there he was, working in a packing shed amongst thousands and thousands of grapefruit and oranges delivered by huge trucks that dumped them on the conveyor belts that carried them through to the other side of the packing shed and put them into boxes and onto other huge trucks that drove them north.

The sounds of conveyor belt after conveyor belt after conveyor belt created a constant rattling roar. Each conveyor belt carried a steady stream of grapefruit or oranges, an unbroken stream of fruit passing by at high speed and bouncing up and down at the same time. Two opposite motions happening simultaneously. As I stared at the thousands of hopping orange dots zooming by, I felt I was seeing pointillism taken to its ultimate mechanical madness.

And there was my father working on the conveyor belts. The conveyor belts included small baths that the fruit passed through on their journey from one side of the shed to the other. The first bath contained chemicals that would instantly wash off the chemicals that had been sprayed on the fruit out in the orchards. The second bath in the conveyor belt system washed off the chemicals that had been used to wash off the chemicals that been sprayed on the fruit out in the orchards, and so on, *ad nauseum* all the way across the shed and into the boxes. After they were cleaned from their many baths, the fruit was sprayed with an infinitesimal fine coating of wax to make them look more orangy and healthy up in Minnesota or Vermont.

My father set up those chemical baths. He mixed the chemicals that made those baths keep running. I could see his hands working.

The day I went with my father to see his new job, I was quite amazed. When we got back into the car between the first and the second packing shed, I was laughing and said to my father that I had never seen him do anything like that. I remembered that when he gave me a gift for Christmas, it would take the two of us until the Fourth of July to get it put together, and there would always be left-over parts. We had quite an intense conversation about his new skill and how amazed I was about it. He beamed with pride, but as the day wore on, and I saw one packing shed after another, I grew bored and saw less and less.

A couple of days later, my father and mother drove me to Winterhaven, Florida, where I could catch a train to Chicago. My mother said goodbye to me in the train station. My father and I walked out onto the train platform to wait for the train. There was only one other man standing in the shade at the opposite end of the platform. It was a hot, sunny Florida afternoon; palm trees; extremely bright light. As we waited, my father and I talked about anything to keep from talking about what was really in our hearts. That was not a part of the "get on back up there" philosophy. And the pain of separation, and our not being able to talk about it was so intense that when the train came, we were actually sort of glad. I got on the train and the older gentleman passed by us, put his hand on my father's shoulder and boarded the train.

I stood in the area between the cars as the train pulled out, and I leaned out and could see my father standing all alone on the train platform waving goodbye to me. Waving goodbye to his youngest son. I thought, *why is it always me pulling out on trains, or buses or cars, or taking off on planes, waving goodbye to the people I love.*

On the train, the old man in the white suit and I were the only two passengers in the car. We started talking. Seems he had just been to a funeral in Winterhaven. He came all the way from Indiana.

"An old friend of yours?" I asked.

"Nope, never met him before in my life."

"Where are you headed?" I asked.

"Chicago," he said.

"To a funeral?" I asked. I had a hunch.

"Yes," he said.

"A friend of yours?"

"Oh, no," he said. And he showed me an itinerary: Funerals, all over the midwest and some out on the northeast coast.

"Friends of yours?" I asked. There must have been a dozen funerals on that list.

"Nope."

"All right," I asked, "I give up; why are you going to all these funerals if you don't know these people?" He got out a pint of Early Times bourbon, we had a couple of drinks, and he told me all about it.

"I'm a veteran," he said, and he took out his discharge papers from World War II. "I retired ten years ago. Wife died five years ago; I live in Ohio, kids grown up, moved away to big cities, nothing to do at home; got kind of blue without my wife there, so I go to veterans' funerals." He showed me an American Legion newspaper, a newsletter or something from the VFW that had information about deaths and funeral notes. "Who knows if every veteran has another veteran at his funeral? Probably not, so I sort of represent the military at these funerals. I think that every veteran should have a veteran at his funeral, and besides I love riding around on trains."

By now we were into the second pint. He told me about the funerals he had been to all over the United States. He told me about his favorite funeral, and he told me about the worst funeral he had ever been to, where the entire funeral he heard people muttering to each other, "Thank God, we're finally getting this son-of-a-bitch buried."

We rolled into Chicago through the south side. Miles of slums. I asked him, "Why do you do this? Isn't it depressing?"

"Oh, no, Jim. Funerals are never depressing. Funerals are my life."

The time I saw my father standing alone on the train platform in Winterhaven, Florida was the last time I ever saw him alive. Winterhaven, Florida: not home to either one of us. He a traveling salesman most of his life, and me, just traveling. We said goodbye in a place of passing for both of us.

At that moment the owl back in the woods outside Rosemount, Minnesota, blinked his eye.

Then I saw my notebooks back on my desk, and·it was very clear to me what was happening. The notebook that was most recent was like my father's handwriting. *Oh yeah*, I thought. *I'm get-*

ting to be more and more like my father all the time, whether I like it or not. My handwriting proves it. The change is sneaking up on me all the time. And for the first time in my life, I liked it. All my life, I did not want to be like my father. Oh, no. He had a steady job, he had car payments, house payments, a wife and kids. He had heavy weights and responsibilities. That was not going to be my life, not for me, oh no. I was going to be "free."

Now here I was in my forties, looking at a letter written to me when my father was in his late fifties, and I could see through our handwriting that we were getting to be more and more alike, whether I liked it or not, and I liked it. He pulled up his roots when he was older than I was; like an immigrant he left Texas. And even though he went only as far away as Florida, it might as well have been Mars. To friends and relatives back in Texas, when you leave Texas you drop right off the face of the planet. They were like immigrants, my parents. And my father learned to work with his hands and that was like changing the DNA of himself.

And if he could do it, and I was getting to be more and more like my father every day, then that meant that in my life if I met an equal challenge, I could do it. And if I could do that, that meant I could do anything.

That's the gift my father was giving me that day back in the packing shed when he showed me himself working with his hands. That's the seed my father planted in me that day.

The owl flew away in the woods back home in Rosemount, Minnesota. The two small birds followed along, calling out, *Eeekkk! Eeekkk! Eeekkk!*

They were quickly out of sight, but I could still hear those little birds calling, still on the job. The call began to fade until all I could hear was the November wind through the bare trees.

I looked at Bear; she looked at me. She said, *Are you ready to go?* I said, "Yeah."

We began walking through the woods again, *dink-t-dink bomp, dink-t-dink bomp, dink-t-dink bomp.*

And I haven't chewed off any of my toes over the years, but I've gotten a few bumps and bruises, and a few crinkles in my walk—so when you watch the two of us walk from behind, it's *dink-t-dink bomp, dink-t-dink bomp, eee-rrr-eee, eee-rrr-eee.*

Not like Bounce and me. Oh Lordy, Bounce and me used to just cruise up and down streets of my hometown, rolling and running. Bear and me, we're *dink-t-dink bomp, dink-t-dink, bomp, eee-rrr-eee, eee-rrr-eee.*

Ol' Bear and me, we ain't crusin', but we're still movin'.

Jim Stowell grew up in McAllen, Texas, in the Rio Grande valley. He has been the co-founder of two theater companies, both created to perform new theater work. Stowell is an actor for stage and screen, as well as an acclaimed director of new theater.

Jim Stowell may also be seen in a live video performance of *Traveling Light*, produced and directed by John Hanson of New Front Films and videotaped on the banks of the Mississippi river. Videocassettes are available from Flower Films, 10341 San Pablo Ave., El Cerrito CA 94530.